Instantly Sweet

75 Desserts
and Sweet Treats
from Your **INSTANT POT®** or Other
ELECTRIC PRESSURE COOKER

Barbara Schieving

AND

Marci Buttars

Fountaindale Public Library
Bolingbrook, IL
(630) 759-2102

Inspiring | Educating | Creating | Entertaining

Brimming with creative inspiration, how-to projects, and useful information to enrich your everyday life, Quarto Knows is a favorite destination for those pursuing their interests and passions. Visit our site and dig deeper with our books into your area of interest: Quarto Creates, Quarto Cooks, Quarto Homes, Quarto Lives, Quarto Drives, Quarto Explores, Quarto Gifts, or Quarto Kids.

22 21 20 19 18   1 2 3 4 5

ISBN: 978-1-55832-937-9

Digital edition published in 2018
eISBN: 978-1-55832-938-6

Library of Congress Cataloging-in-Publication Data available.

Design and Page Layout: Megan Jones Design
Cover Image: Barbara Schieving
Photography: Barbara Schieving and Marci Buttars

Printed in China

MIX
Paper from
responsible sources
FSC® C104723

To our families, friends, and readers, who share our love of food and have supported us in exploring the exciting possibilities of pressure cooking.

Contents

Sweet Wishes: Notes from the Authors   6

Sweet Talk: Making Desserts in Your Electric Pressure Cooker   7

Sweet Tricks: Tips for Getting Great Results   11

Sweet Stuff: Specialty Equipment   18

Bittersweet Moments: Troubleshooting Guide   20

* **Quick Breads and Breakfasts**   23

* **Cheesecakes**   39

* **Lava Cakes**   59

* **Cakes**   75

* **Pies**   89

* **Cobblers and Fruit Desserts**   107

* **Custards and Puddings**   117

* **Sauces, Fillings, and Toppings**   131

Acknowledgments   156

About the Authors   157

Index   158

Sweet Wishes

Notes from the Authors

Desserts have always been my favorite thing to cook. I can't help it—they're also my favorite thing to eat! Over the years, I've collected notebooks full of family-favorite recipes for every occasion.

Of course, when I fell in love with pressure cooking, I had to try making something to satisfy my sweet tooth. One of the first recipes I adapted was a rice pudding that I've been making for thirty years. In the pressure cooker, it came out richer and creamier than ever before, and it was *so* easy to cook.

From that moment on, I was hooked.

I can't wait for you to see how easy it is to make delicious desserts for your next baby shower or family get-together—or just a little something to celebrate the end of a long day.

—Barbara Schieving

My excitement for cooking began at a very early age and was centered on desserts for several years. My mother was in charge of dinner and I was responsible for making all the treats—did I ever love my job!

Fast-forward several years and I now have my own family that is equally happy to help me create delicious, memorable desserts. Sweets and treats have an impressive ability to bring smiles to people's faces and joy to a room!

My love of all things pressure cooking runs deep, and it was only a matter of time before these two loves combined. Desserts made in a pressure cooker are absolutely amazing—the textures and depth of flavor are on a whole new delicious level, and the cooking process is often easier and faster!

You will discover so many impressive and delicious desserts and learn new cooking techniques as you cook your way through this book! May it bring much joy into your lives as well!

—Marci Buttars

Sweet Talk

Making Desserts in Your Electric Pressure Cooker

WHY PRESSURE COOK DESSERTS?

Electric pressure cookers have been a hot-ticket item for a few years now, as people have discovered how to make fast and flavorful meals in these appliances. However, electric pressure cookers are capable of so much more than cooking Sunday dinner!

When you use your electric pressure cooker to make desserts, you'll notice the following advantages:

Better taste. Some desserts just taste better when they're cooked in an electric pressure cooker. Any dessert that's best cooked in a moist environment, such as a water bath, is a perfect match for the pressure cooker. For example, the steamy environment inside your pressure cooker creates a super-creamy cheesecake that cooks evenly. Desserts "baked" in the pressure cooker are much more forgiving than those baked in the oven and won't dry out as easily.

Quicker cook times. This hallmark of pressure cooking applies to desserts as well. Cheesecakes, puddings, pies, and so many other favorites are ready in a fraction of the time compared to those conventionally prepared.

Cool cooking. In the heat of summer, no one wants to turn on the oven. Desserts made in the electric pressure cooker offer a wide variety of sweet treats without heating up the house.

Hands-off convenience. Instead of standing at the stove babysitting a sauce or pie filling, stirring constantly, with an electric pressure cooker, you start the pressure cooker and walk away. How easy is that?

Automatic portion control. Because desserts made in the electric pressure cooker have to fit inside the pressure cooking pot, the recipes often call for smaller pans and reduced ingredient amounts. This smaller size leads to automatic portion control. Instead of a cake that serves twelve to sixteen people, we have cake recipes that serve two, four, six, or eight—just enough to satisfy that sweet tooth without leftovers to tempt you for more.

Cute and fun. The pot-in-pot method of cooking desserts in the electric pressure cooker lends itself to using cute and fun smaller-size containers, such as Mason jars, ramekins, and Bundt pans. These desserts come out of the pressure cooker party-ready.

GETTING TO KNOW YOUR PRESSURE COOKER

While there are a lot of different parts and buttons, your pressure cooker is actually pretty simple to use when you get to know it. Read the user manual that comes with it for details on your particular model; however, note that all brands of electric pressure cookers are made of similar parts. For your convenience, we've included a quick explanation.

Housing. This is the outer part of the pressure cooker—the one with the buttons and the heating element inside. *Do not* add ingredients directly to the housing; you may damage your pressure cooker.

Cooking pot. The inner removable pot is made of stainless steel, ceramic, or nonstick aluminum, depending on your brand, and it's where the magic happens. While adding the ingredients to this pot, you can treat it just like a pot on the stove—for example, lift it up away from the heat to slow the cooking when thickening sauces. Once you lock the lid in place and bring the pot to pressure, however, you'll be unable to access this pot until the pressure is released.

Lid. All electric pressure cookers have a lid with a handle, valve, and mechanism to release the steam on the exterior and a place to attach the sealing ring underneath.

Pressure release valve/button. This plastic piece is located on the lid's exterior and controls whether the pressure inside the pot can escape. (Depending on your model of electric pressure cooker, you will have either a valve or a button to release the steam.) Use it to seal the electric pressure cooker and release the steam quickly.

Sealing ring. This removable ring attaches to the underside of the lid and is made of tough, food-grade silicone. When the lid is locked in place, this ring seals the pressure cooker so air cannot escape, allowing the machine to build pressure inside the pot.

Float valve. This small valve fits inside the lid and is paired with a miniature silicone gasket. When your electric pressure cooker reaches pressure, steam pushes the float valve up and seals the cooker. In this raised position, the lid locks and cannot be opened until the valve drops again when the pressure is released.

Choosing a Button

Some pressure cookers are very basic, having just two buttons: High Pressure and Cancel. Other electric pressure cookers, also known as multi-cookers, have multiple buttons and many pressure cooking levels. While your user manual will have an in-depth explanation of these buttons, there is one principle that holds true no matter what button you choose: *The buttons are generally preset cook times for different foods; your pressure cooker* cannot *sense what you are actually cooking and* cannot *tell you when the food is cooked.*

The recipes in this cookbook were developed using just two buttons:

High Pressure/Manual/Pressure Cook: The precise name of this button depends on the model of electric pressure cooker you own. When a recipe says, "Select High Pressure and 5 minutes cook time," this will be the button you use. (If your pressure cooker doesn't have a manual button, consult the user manual and use the preset button with the closest time to the cook time in the recipe.

White Chocolate Macadamia Lava Cake, page 71

For example, on the Power Pressure Cooker XL, you'd select the Bean/Lentil button, which has a 5-minute cook time, corresponding to the 5 minutes of cook time called for in the recipe.)

Sauté/Simmer/Browning: Use this button with the lid *off*. It's used with desserts for melting butter or thickening sauces. Depending on your brand of electric pressure cooker, you may have separate buttons for each heat level or a single button that can adjust the heat level up or down as desired. Some brands don't have a Sauté button, and users select a preset button, such as Chicken, and use the cooker with the lid off.

In addition, there are two other buttons you need to know about:

Keep Warm: When the cook time ends, many electric pressure cookers do not turn the heat off entirely and automatically switch to the Keep Warm setting. This setting is useful; however, the contents of the pot will continue to cook as long as the Keep Warm setting is on, so make sure to turn off the pressure cooker when you're done using it.

Yogurt: Many electric pressure cookers use the Yogurt button on High to pasteurize milk, and adjust to Normal for incubating yogurt. You can make yogurt in the pressure cooker without the button, but the steps will be different than the recipe included in this cookbook.

LEARNING THE RECIPE TERMINOLOGY

While many of you may be familiar with pressure cooking terminology, for those of you who (like Barbara) want to start with making dessert first, here's a brief guide to help you get ready to cook with confidence.

Once the cook time ends, the timer will sound. At this point, the recipe will direct you to release the pressure using one of the following methods:

Quick pressure release: A *quick pressure release* does exactly what it says—when the cook time ends, turn the pressure release valve to Venting and watch the jet of steam shoot out of the pressure release valve. When venting, avoid placing your face or hands directly over the valve, as the steam is hot and can burn, and be sure to position your pressure cooker so the steam vents away from your cabinets. If liquid or foam starts coming out of the pressure release valve, flip the valve back to the Sealed position for a minute or two and then try releasing the pressure again. Wait until the pressure is completely released, the float valve drops, and the lid unlocks easily before you carefully open the lid.

Natural pressure release: In comparison, a *natural pressure release* is a bit anticlimactic—when the cook time ends, just leave the pressure release valve in the Sealed position. The pressure releases slowly through the valve, with no visible jet of steam or noise coming from the pot. With this method, the only way you'll know the pressure is fully released is the float valve will drop and the lid will unlock easily.

Some recipes combine the two, instructing you to do a natural pressure release for a certain amount of time, and finish with a quick pressure release. With this system, simply wait the specified number of minutes before turning the valve from Sealed to Venting to release any remaining pressure.

PERFORMING A PRACTICE TEST

If you're completely new to electric pressure cooking, use the classic "water test" to become familiar with it before you start cooking with food.

1. Add 1 cup (235 ml) of water to the pressure cooking pot and carefully place the pot inside the housing.

2. Check that the lid has the sealing ring in place. Close and lock the lid and ensure the pressure release valve is in the Sealed position.

3. Select High Pressure using the Manual/Pressure Cook button and set 5 minutes cook time. (Note the timer won't start counting down until the pot reaches pressure, which may take another 5 minutes.)

4. When the timer sounds, carefully turn the pressure release valve to the Venting position so steam can escape and the pressure can release. The steam will be hot and can burn, so keep your hands and face away from the valve.

5. Once the steam disperses completely, the lid will unlock. Carefully remove the lid, tilting it so the steam in the pot vents away from you. Use hot pads or silicone mitts to remove the hot cooking pot from the housing. Don't forget to turn off the pressure cooker!

Sweet Tricks

Tips for Getting Great Results

Desserts made in a pressure cooker are fabulous—the textures and flavors are on a completely new delicious level, and the cooking process is often easier and faster!

Pressure cooking desserts can require an adjustment in approach—unlike oven cooking, you can't see or touch the dessert while it's cooking. However, just like everything else you do in your kitchen, after a little practice, you'll be a pro. Here are a few tips and tricks specific to cooking desserts that will help you as you learn the ropes.

Tested in a 6-quart (5.7 L) pressure cooker: All recipes in this cookbook were created and tested using a 6-quart (5.7 L) electric pressure cooker. They will work in larger pressure cookers, but your cook times may be slightly different and you may need to put more water underneath the dessert pan.

Read the entire recipe: Many dessert recipes, such as cheesecakes, take a short amount of time in the pressure cooker but chill several hours to overnight before they're ready to serve. To increase your success level, read the entire recipe and have the ingredients measured and chopped prior to cooking.

Trust your senses: If something seems off, listen to your intuition. Remove the cooking pot from the housing if you smell something burning or use a quick pressure release and remove the lid if you see steam escaping from the sides while cooking.

Pot-in-pot cooking: Many of the dessert recipes are made using the pot-in-pot method of pressure cooking. Pot-in-pot cooking is easy to do. All you're doing is putting a pot on a trivet above some liquid. The liquid creates the steam necessary to create the pressure and cook your dessert.

Doubling recipes: Many of the dessert recipes in this cookbook, such as cheesecakes and cakes, cannot be doubled. However, some recipes, such as the rice pudding and breakfast risotto, are easily doubled with no change in cook time. Just be sure your pot isn't more than two-thirds full. For foods that foam, such as berry compotes, do not fill your pot more than halfway and be sure to increase the natural pressure release time by at least 5 minutes.

Measuring flour: The way you measure flour can make a big difference in the end result of a recipe. Fluff the flour in the canister before measuring it, and use a scoop to fill the measuring cup. When the cup is full, use the back of the scoop or a knife to level the flour.

Measuring sugar: For granulated sugar and powdered sugar, use a scoop to fill the measuring cup and level it off. For brown sugar, press the sugar firmly to pack it into the measuring cup.

Measuring salt: Develop the habit of measuring salt away from the other ingredients in your cooking bowl. This saves you from accidental spills!

Separating eggs: Use this trick to quickly separate the egg white from the egg yolk: Crack the egg into your hand over a bowl. Separate your fingers slightly, and the white will fall into the bowl while you gently cradle the yolk in your hand. Transfer the yolk to a separate bowl, or add to your mixing bowl as needed.

Heavy whipping cream: When a recipe calls for heavy whipping cream, do not use regular whipping cream or ultra-pasteurized heavy cream. Regular whipping cream has a lower amount of milk fat, and while ultra-pasteurized heavy cream has a longer shelf life, it doesn't whip as easily or hold its shape as long as a traditional pasteurized heavy whipping cream.

Butter: We use *unsalted butter* in our recipes. The amount of salt can vary among brands, so we prefer to use unsalted for consistent flavor.

Full-fat cream cheese: For best results, use full-fat cream cheese. You can substitute Neufchâtel (one-third less fat), but we don't recommend using fat-free cream cheese.

Freshly squeezed juices: Use freshly squeezed orange, lemon, or lime juice for best flavor.

QUICK BREADS AND BREAKFASTS

Make and freeze: Many of these quick breads and breakfasts freeze well. For breakfasts like steel cut oats and risottos, we like to freeze them in zip-top bags in individual servings so it's easy to reheat only as many servings as you need.

Slice quick breads and breakfast cakes before freezing: We like to slice quick breads and breakfast cakes before freezing so they thaw more quickly. A slice of frozen bread will be thawed by lunchtime—a perfect treat for lunchboxes!

Change up your flavors: Steel cut oats, risotto, and yogurt are blank slates—adapt these recipes to incorporate your favorite flavors.

CHEESECAKES

Use room temperature ingredients: The key to making perfect pressure cooker cheesecake is having the ingredients at room temperature. The easiest way to soften cream cheese is to leave it on your counter at room temperature for several hours. However, if you forget, put the cream cheese in a zip-top bag and place it in warm (not hot) water for about 15 minutes. Add the eggs to the warm water, and they'll be at room temperature in about 5 minutes.

Keep the crust low: Don't press your crumbs too high up the side of the springform pan. Crumbs pressed too high may lead to moisture in your crust.

Use a sling: A sling makes it so easy to lower the cheesecake into the pot and to lift the hot cheesecake back out of the pressure cooker. You can make your own sling out of a folded 26 × 4-inch (66 × 10 cm) strip of aluminum foil or you can purchase a silicone sling just for pressure cooking.

Know your timing: Timing can vary based on a variety of factors, including altitude, type of pan used, and the ingredients. Typically, cheesecakes require longer cook times at higher altitudes. Recipes that call for mix-ins, such as candy or chocolate chips, also require a longer cook time. If you cover your pan with aluminum foil, add at least 5 minutes to the total cook time. You may also find you prefer to cook your cheesecakes a little longer to achieve a denser New York–style texture.

Check the temperature: Because cheesecakes are supposed to come out a little jiggly in the middle, it can be hard to tell when they're done. Use an instant read thermometer to check that the cheesecake has reached 150°F (65.5°C) in the center. If it's not quite there, cook the cheesecake at High Pressure for an additional 5 minutes, using a second 10-minute natural pressure release.

Remove water from the top: Sometimes steam collects on the lid and drips onto the cheesecake while it's cooking. Once you've removed the cheesecake from the inner pot, use the corner of a paper towel to carefully absorb the liquid from the top of the cheesecake.

Remove from the pan: Allow your cheesecake to cool for several hours or overnight before removing it from the pan. Heat a flat metal spatula under hot running water. Wipe dry with a towel and carefully run the warm spatula along the sides of the springform pan to loosen any remaining cheesecake from the pan. Carefully open the springform pan. Use a long (10 inches, or 25 cm, or longer) flat metal spatula along the bottom of the cheesecake to separate it from the pan. Carefully transfer the cheesecake to the serving dish.

Fix cracks: Even in the moist environment of the pressure cooker, your cheesecake can crack along the top. If topping your cheesecake with a sauce or compote, this might not matter, but if you're serving it naked, you can fix it. Heat a thin metal spatula under hot running water, wipe it dry, and carefully spread the top of the cheesecake in short, slow strokes until the crack starts to fill. Continue until you're happy with the appearance.

Use easy storage: A reader came up with this ingenious way to store and transport a 7-inch (18 cm) cheesecake: Find a large round container that is at least 8 inches (20 cm) in diameter and at least 3 inches (7.5 cm) deep. (I use a disposable plastic container from my local grocery store.) After the cheesecake has cooled in the refrigerator, remove it from the pan and place it on the lid of the container. (Be sure you have the lid turned the right way.) Carefully lower the container over the cheesecake and snap tightly in place. The lid becomes the plate and the bowl becomes the cake dome.

LAVA CAKES

Cook three ramekins at a time: These recipes are written to cook three lava cakes first and let those rest while you pressure cook the remaining three lava cakes for the best, most consistent results. If you want to cook fewer than three at a time, your cakes are likely to be undercooked. Solve this by using three ramekins in the pot and filling any empty ones with water. (Similarly, if you're cooking in an 8-quart [7.5 L] pressure cooker, use four ramekins and fill any unused ones with water.)

Cook six ramekins at a time: If you're in a hurry and want to cook all six at once, use a short rack and a tall rack to stack them so there is at least 1 inch (2.5 cm) of space between the ramekins to allow the cakes to rise as they cook, produce consistent molten lava results, and reduce the chances of overcooking.

Measure carefully: Use exactly 1 cup (235 ml) of lukewarm water in the pot under the trivet, and use a cook time of 4 minutes at High Pressure with a quick pressure release.

Make ahead: You can make the lava cake batter up to three days in advance. Follow the recipe to where you divide the batter into six 6-ounce (175 ml) ramekins. Do not add the truffle or filling to the centers. Cover and refrigerate. When you're ready to cook, let the ramekins sit out for 1 hour or so until they reach room temperature. Add the centers and cook according to the recipe instructions.

Check for doneness: The sides of the cakes should be set and the center slightly soft. If the cake is overcooked, it will still be fudgy or moist and delicious, but it won't have the molten filling. If you think the cake is under-cooked, add 1 minute of cook time at High Pressure if the sides are slightly set, and 2 minutes if all the batter is still quite loose.

CAKES

Start with a cake mix: Many recipes in this cookbook use cake mixes. We love cooking from scratch whenever possible, but boxed cake mixes contain emulsifiers that often produce better results than from-scratch cakes when cooked at the lower tempera-tures inside the electric pressure cooker. In our experience, making cake mix cakes in the pressure cooker results in a lighter, fluffier cake. If you're hoping to adapt your favorite cake recipe to the pressure cooker, we recommend starting with a cake mix.

Make homemade icing: While in a pinch you can grab a tub of frosting from your local grocery store, homemade icings are easy to make and taste so much better than store-bought frosting. Don't be afraid to give them a try!

Switch up the toppings: Make these cakes your own by switching up the toppings and sauces; for example, top the Angel Food Cake (page 77) with Dark Chocolate Syrup (page 136) or fresh fruit drizzled in Crème Anglaise (page 143).

PIES

Precook pie filling: When you precook your fruit filling, you'll know exactly how much thickener the fruit needs, and you'll serve picture-perfect slices. The filling is cooked and ready in less than 10 minutes and you don't have to worry about cutting into the pie and having all the juices run out.

Make ahead: There's nothing like hot pie, fresh out of the oven. As many of these reci-pes use prebaked piecrusts, they're perfect to make ahead and fill right before eating.

Triple Layer Chocolate Mint Cheesecake, page 50

Change up the crust: Many piecrusts are interchangeable—switch them up to meet your tastes! For example, with Strawberry Pie (page 101), you can use a traditional dough crust, or opt for a graham cracker or Oreo crust, depending on your mood or what's on hand.

Make perfect piecrusts: If you prefer an old-fashioned, super-flaky piecrust, you'll want to make it from scratch. Here are Barbara's tips for perfect piecrusts:

- *Keep it cold at every stage.* The secret to a tender, flaky piecrust is keeping all the ingredients really cold. (If making the dough in a food processor, you can even freeze the fat before using.) Chill the dough in the refrigerator for at least 30 minutes before rolling it out. Once rolled, transfer it to the pie plate and chill for another 30 minutes before filling or baking.

- *Use a mix of butter and shortening.* For me, the perfect piecrust uses a mixture of butter and shortening. You get flakiness from the shortening and rich taste from the butter.

- *Don't overmix.* I prefer to mix my dough with a pastry cutter; if you use a food processer, be careful not to overprocess it! You want pea-size pieces of fat.

- *Choose the right pie pan.* For a browned bottom crust, use a dark metal or heatproof glass pie pan. Shiny pans deflect heat from the pie so the crust doesn't brown and crisp well. (If using shiny or thin pans, place the pans on a cookie sheet to bake.)

- *Use plastic wrap for rolling.* If you've never gotten the hang of rolling out dough on a floured surface, or if you don't want to incorporate more flour into the dough while rolling, try plastic wrap instead. Roll the dough between two sheets of plastic

wrap side by side on the bottom and two more on top—straighten the plastic when necessary. Putting the bottom plastic wrap on a silicone baking mat helps keep it from moving while you're rolling the dough. Peel off the top sheet of plastic and pick up the bottom sheet of plastic with the dough on it and flip it over into your pie plate. Peel the bottom sheet of plastic off after the dough is fitted into the pie plate. Try each method, plastic wrap and a floured surface, to see which one you prefer.

- *Handle the dough carefully.* Roll the dough from the center outward using even, firm rolls. Turn the dough as you work; about an eighth of a turn for each roll will help keep it round. When fitting dough in the pie plate, don't stretch the dough, or it will shrink back as it bakes. Press the dough gently against the sides and bottom of the pan to keep air from getting trapped between the dough and the pan.

- *Patch the crust.* Don't worry if your piecrust tears. It's no big deal and patching is easy. Roll a scrap of dough a little larger than the damaged area. Trim the edges, dampen them lightly with water, and place the patch, damp side-down, over the break. Seal by gently pressing the edges of the patch with your fingers.

- *Brown the crust.* Brush the bottom and sides of the unbaked piecrust with a lightly beaten egg white to help the crust brown.

- *Use a hot oven.* High heat explodes solid fat particles (chilling the dough hardens the fat). The explosions create steam, which lightens and crisps the pastry. At lower oven temperatures, the fat just softens and melts. If there's no explosion, there's no steam— and the pie crust won't be flaky.

COBBLERS AND FRUIT DESSERTS

Fresh or frozen. Feel free to substitute fresh fruit for frozen or vice versa when pressure cooking fruit desserts. Frozen fruit is often frozen at its peak of ripeness and is usually a better choice when fresh fruit isn't at its best.

Mix it up. The fruit can be switched up in many of these recipes to match your flavor preferences or what's in season.

Nice and thick: Some fruit is juicier than others and may need additional thickening. Simply whisk 1 tablespoon (8 g) cornstarch with 1 tablespoon (15 ml) cold water and add the resulting cornstarch slurry to the fruit in the cooking pot, stirring constantly.

CUSTARDS AND PUDDINGS

Choose the right rice for the pudding. The rice pudding recipes call for arborio rice, which produces a creamy, delicious rice pudding. In a pinch, you can substitute regular long-grain white rice, which cooks in the same amount of time. However, the final product won't be as creamy, so you may want to add a bit of cream along with the milk.

Try a milk substitute. You can use milk substitutes, such as almond, rice, or coconut milk, or use half-and-half, or skim milk in these recipes. However, be aware that the more fat there is in the milk or cream, the creamier the dishes will set up in the fridge.

Stir some milk or cream into the pudding the next day to bring it back to the perfect creaminess. If you're using a milk with less fat, you may want to add an extra egg yolk to thicken the pudding or custard.

Use a nonstick pot. When making tapioca pudding in the pressure cooker, we prefer to use a nonstick pot for best results. (If your brand of electric pressure cooker didn't come with a nonstick pot, you may be able to order one.)

SAUCES, FILLINGS, AND TOPPINGS

Stretch your berries: If you don't quite have enough berries to make the recipe, you can add a diced apple to the berries. It gives the compote more structure and volume.

Consider evaporated vs. sweetened condensed milk: When cooking Dulce de Leche (page 146), remember that evaporated milk and sweetened condensed milk are not interchangeable. Be sure to use sweetened condensed milk with this recipe.

Using the Sauté button: For sauces using the Sauté button, if the inner pot is getting too hot and you're worried about scorching the sauce, simply lift the pot a few inches (centimeters) to increase the distance between the pot and the heating element, stirring constantly. (You may want to use an oven mitt for this, as the inner pot can get hot.)

Lower the heat: Many of these sauces do best when cooked at a simmer or using the Sauté button adjusted to low. If your sauce thickens too quickly, lift the pot away from the heating element while stirring constantly.

Sweet Stuff

Specialty Equipment

So much of cooking revolves around using the right equipment! Pressure cooking is the same: The right equipment is any oven-safe dish that fits inside the pressure cooking pot when placed on a trivet. You likely already have many of these may around your house and, if not, most are very affordable.

All items listed here are used in this cookbook and are recommended for use in a 6-quart (5.7 L) pressure cooker. As a general rule, 6-quart (5.7 L) pressure cookers can usually fit a 7-inch (18 cm) pan; 8-quart (7.5 L) pressure cookers can usually fit an 8-inch (20 cm) pan, and 3-quart (2.8 L) pressure cookers can usually fit a 6-inch (15 cm) pan. However, those of you with larger or smaller pressure cookers will need to measure to see what fits in your pressure cooking pot; just make sure it's not too tight of a fit—you need enough room around the sides for the steam to rise and build pressure.

Springform pan: If you want to make cheesecake in the pressure cooker, we recommend a leak-proof 7-inch (18 cm) springform pan. Some people like to use a PushPan to make cheesecakes instead of a springform pan; while we prefer a springform pan, a PushPan works well, too.

Round cake pan: A 7-inch (18 cm) round cake pan is a workhorse in your pressuring cooker arsenal. It's used for making cakes, bread puddings, and other delicious sweets. The Chocolate-Raspberry Cake for Two (page 80) uses tiny 4-inch (10 cm) round cake pans.

Half-size Bundt pan: A half-size (6-cup, or 1.4 L) Bundt pan without a large rim fits perfectly in a 6-quart (5.7 L) pressure cooker. This pan allows certain desserts to cook more quickly and evenly than in a simple cake pan. (Bonus: Desserts made in a half-size pan fit perfectly in a gallon-size [23 L] zip-top bag for freezing or sharing.)

Angel food cake pan: If you really love angel food cake and plan to make it a lot, this pan is worth the investment. Otherwise, we think you can get results almost as good from the half-size Bundt pan.

Glass custard cups: These small glass cups are convenient for cooking single-serve desserts such as the Oreo–Chocolate Chip Mini Cheesecakes (page 55). Up to six 6-ounce (175 ml) custard cups will fit, stacked three on three.

Porcelain stacking ramekins: Up to six 5-ounce (150 ml) ramekins will fit, stacked three on three. You will need two trivets, a short one and a tall one, to make six at a time.

Yogurt maker: Also called a *yogurt strainer kit*, this utensil consists of a fine-mesh strainer that sits inside a larger bowl to catch the whey as it drains. We consider it essential to making thick, creamy yogurt in the electric pressure cooker. If you prefer, you can use nut milk bags or large coffee filters.

Mason jars: Made to withstand high heat, Mason jars of various sizes work wonderfully in the electric pressure cooker. Recipes in this book use 4-ounce (120 ml), 8-ounce (235 ml), and 16-ounce (475 ml) Mason jars.

Trivet: This simple accessory keeps ingredients away from the cooking liquid and the heating element on the bottom of the pot. Sometimes called a *rack*, trivets come in various heights. We recommend two or three different styles to allow you to stack containers.

Extra silicone ring: When cooking delicately flavored desserts, we feel it's important to use a silicone ring that is not infused with the smell of strong savory foods, like Saturday night's chili. (There are dozens of ways to clean the silicone ring, but we haven't yet found one that completely gets rid of the smell of strong foods.)

Sling: Many recipes in this book use a sling to make it easier to remove pots and pans from the cooking pot. In all recipes in this book that use a sling, fold down the sling so the lid will lock. You can make your own sling by folding aluminum foil into a strip that's 26 inches (66 cm) long and 4 inches (10 cm) wide. Or cut a large silicone pastry mat into similarly sized strips or use specialty items such as silicone bands that stretch around the pan.

Canning jar lifter tongs: This little tool makes it easy to remove all sizes of canning jars from the electric pressure cooker.

Retriever tongs: When doing pot-in-pot cooking, these little helpers let you get a good grip on the pot so it's easier to remove.

Instant-read thermometer: For desserts such as cheesecakes that aren't quite set when fully cooked, an instant-read thermometer makes it easy to tell whether what's in your pot needs a little more cook time. It doesn't matter whether it's a fork-style or pen-style thermometer, as long as it gives a numerical temperature reading.

Silicone mini-mitts: An inexpensive set of flexible silicone mitts is the perfect accessory for lifting a hot inner pot out of the housing or for gripping the inner pot while you stir your food. (An all-silicone design is easy to clean, too!)

Tamper: This little wooden tool is a big time-saver for making cheesecake crusts. You can use the bottom of a glass to press the crust firmly into the bottom of the pan as well if you don't have one.

Bittersweet Moments

Troubleshooting Guide

Once in a while, something goes wrong—it happens even to the best cooks! Readers of our blogs and our families and friends often ask what they can do to save the dish. The following are some of their most common questions and our recommendations to address those concerns.

My pot didn't come to pressure. There are a couple of reasons your pot won't come to pressure. First, check to be sure you have a good seal from the gasket. A common problem is that the silicone gasket is not inserted properly, allowing steam to escape from the sides. Also check that the float valve is in place and the pressure release valve is turned to the Sealed position. Confirm there is enough liquid in the pot. Most pressure cookers require 1 cup (235 ml) of liquid to come to pressure. Certain ingredients release liquid when they cook, so some recipes may call for less to start. However, if you are using a larger pressure cooker, you may need to add more liquid to bring your pot to pressure.

My pudding burned on the bottom. Many sauces need to simmer at a low temperature, so you will have best results if your pressure cooker allows you to adjust the temperature to a low setting. If it does not adjust to low, consider cooking the pudding in a separate pot on the stove. If the pudding overheats while cooking, lift the pot a few inches (centimeters) above the heating element while stirring constantly.

My ganache is too thin or too thick. Ganache thickens as it cools. To speed the thickening process, put the ganache in the fridge to cool. If it gets too thick, you can always heat it in the microwave at medium power in 30-second intervals until it thins a little.

My frosting is lumpy. If you're making a frosting or glaze that includes powdered sugar, you can use an electric mixer to beat the icing until it's smooth.

My cake stuck to the pan. Coat your pans well with nonstick cooking spray, or baking spray with flour, and use a paper towel to spread the spray evenly around the pan. Let the cake cool in the pan for at least 5 minutes before trying to unmold it. If necessary, use a thin spatula to separate the cake from the edge of the pan.

My dessert is undercooked. With cheesecakes, it is easy to tell if they are undercooked: The middle should register 150°F (65.5°C) with an instant-read thermometer. With lava cakes, the sides should be set and the center slightly soft. If they need to be cooked a little longer, relock the lid and cook at High Pressure for a few minutes more—the exact time may vary from recipe to recipe.

My whipped cream is overwhipped. If your cream is overwhipped, don't throw it out—you might be able to save it. Add a few more tablespoons (about 45 ml) of heavy cream to the overwhipped cream. Then, using a wire whisk, gently mix until smooth and creamy.

My cheesecake is not smooth. The main cause of lumpy cheesecake is not using room-temperature ingredients. Ideally, all ingredients should sit on the counter for several hours before mixing. In a pinch, you can place the cream cheese in a zip-top bag and then place the bag and the eggs in a bowl of lukewarm water for 15 minutes.

Overmixing the cheesecake batter adds too much air to the cheesecake and can cause the batter to flow over the sides of the pan and give the cheesecake an odd cottage cheese–like texture.

My compote turned out watery. Watery compotes are easily fixed. In a small bowl, stir together 1 tablespoon (8 g) cornstarch and 1 tablespoon (15 ml) water. Add this slurry to the compote in the cooking pot. Select Sauté and cook, stirring constantly, until the compote thickens.

My piecrust is too dry. If making piecrust from scratch and the dough won't hold together when pressed into a ball, stir in an extra tablespoon (15 ml) of water or (15 g) of sour cream.

My fruit filling is too tart. Taste your fruit. If it is very tart, add a little more sugar before cooking.

My pudding has white pieces in it. This sometimes happens when the eggs are not fully incorporated into the milk. Next time, beat the eggs well into the milk and strain the pudding mixture before cooking it. This will give you a smoother pudding.

My yogurt isn't smooth. The smoothness of the yogurt depends on the fat content of the milk you use. The recipe calls for 2 percent milk, which results in a nice smooth yogurt. Whole milk results in extra-smooth, rich, and creamy yogurt that doubles as dessert. Skim milk, or 1 percent milk, may be used, but will result in a thinner yogurt that isn't as smooth.

My bread pudding turned out too watery or too dry. The type of bread you use makes a big difference in how your bread pudding turns out. Some breads don't absorb as much liquid and won't puff up as much when baked, so if you're using a different type of bread than the recipe calls for, adjust the liquids accordingly.

Quick Breads and Breakfasts

These quick breads and breakfasts are perfect when you want a little something special to start your day on a sweet note.

▶ **Cinnamon Roll Steel Cut Oats**   **24**

▶ **Orange-Cranberry Breakfast Risotto**   **25**

▶ **Honey Vanilla Greek Yogurt**   **26**

▶ **Brown Sugar Banana Nut Bread**   **28**

▶ **Pineapple Upside-Down Breakfast Cake**   **29**

▶ **Carrot Cake Breakfast Cake with Cream Cheese Yogurt Frosting**   **31**

▶ **Honey Orange Poppy Seed Breakfast Cake with Raspberry-Orange Sauce**   **32**

▶ **Pumpkin-Chocolate Chip Breakfast Cake**   **34**

▶ **Sweet Peach Raspberry Swirl Breakfast Cake**   **35**

▶ **Overnight Cinnamon-Pecan Monkey Bread**   **36**

◀ Overnight Cinnamon-Pecan Monkey Bread, page 36

CINNAMON ROLL STEEL CUT OATS

Steel cut oats made with the flavors of a cinnamon roll—a brown sugar–cinnamon topping and a swirl of rich cream cheese icing. A sweet start to the day that's also loaded with good-for-you fiber.

FOR STEEL CUT OATS

1 tablespoon (14 g) butter

1 cup (176 g) steel cut oats

3½ cups (823 ml) water

¼ teaspoon salt

¾ cup (110 g) raisins

FOR BROWN SUGAR TOPPING

¼ cup (60 g) packed light brown sugar

1 teaspoon ground cinnamon

FOR CREAM CHEESE ICING

2 ounces (55 g) cream cheese, at room temperature

2 tablespoons (15 g) powdered sugar, plus more as needed

1 teaspoon milk, plus more as needed

To make the steel cut oats: Select Sauté and melt the butter in the pressure cooking pot. Add the oats. Toast, stirring constantly, until the oats start to darken and smell nutty, about 3 minutes. Add the water and salt to the cooking pot. Lock the lid in place and turn the pressure release valve to the Sealed position. Select High Pressure and 10 minutes cook time.

When the cook time ends, turn off the pressure cooker. Let the pressure release naturally for 5 minutes, and finish with a quick pressure release. When the valve drops, carefully remove the lid. Stir the oats, then stir in the raisins. Cover and let sit until the oats are your desired thickness, 5 to 10 minutes.

To make the brown sugar topping: In a small bowl, stir together the brown sugar and cinnamon.

To make the cream cheese icing: In another small bowl, whisk the cream cheese, powdered sugar, and milk. Add more milk or powdered sugar as necessary to make an icing that will swirl.

Serve in individual bowls sprinkled with the brown sugar topping and a swirl of cream cheese icing.

YIELD: 4 servings

> **TIP:** For me, a great cinnamon roll has to have raisins; if you're not a fan, omit them.

- ▸ PREP TIME: 5 minutes
- ▸ COOK TIME: 6 minutes
- ▸ TOTAL TIME: 20 minutes

ORANGE-CRANBERRY BREAKFAST RISOTTO

If you love rice pudding, try this breakfast risotto. While similar to rice pudding, it has less fat and sugar.

2 tablespoons (28 g) unsalted butter, melted

1½ cups (270 g) arborio rice

3 cups (705 ml) water

Juice of 1 orange (about ½ cup, or 120 ml)

Zest of 1 orange

⅓ cup (67 g) sugar

¼ teaspoon salt

½ cup (60 g) dried cranberries

½ cup (120 ml) milk, plus more for serving (see Tip)

Brown sugar, for serving

Nuts, for serving

Select Sauté and melt the butter in the pressure cooking pot. Stir in the rice and cook for 3 to 4 minutes, stirring frequently, until the rice becomes opaque. Stir in the water, orange juice and zest, sugar, and salt. Lock the lid in place and turn the pressure release valve to the Sealed position. Select High Pressure and 6 minutes cook time.

When the cook time ends, turn off the pressure cooker. Let the pressure release naturally for 2 minutes, and finish with a quick pressure release. When the valve drops, carefully remove the lid. Stir in the cranberries and milk. If necessary, select Sauté and cook the rice for 1 to 2 minutes until it's the consistency you like.

Serve topped with brown sugar, nuts, and a splash of milk.

YIELD: 6 servings

> ▸ **TIP:** For a richer, creamier risotto, substitute ½ cup (120 ml) heavy cream for the milk. This dish tastes great the next day! Be sure to add more milk before you rewarm it to get that creamy consistency back.

- PREP: 5 minutes
- INCUBATE: 8 hours
- CHILL: 6 hours, or overnight
- STRAIN: 24 hours

HONEY VANILLA GREEK YOGURT

Homemade yogurt tastes better than store-bought—and it's much cheaper! This honey vanilla Greek yogurt is so thick and luxurious you will happily eat it as dessert, too!

1 gallon (3.8 L) whole milk

¼ cup (60 g) plain Greek yogurt with live active cultures

½ cup (170 g) honey

1 to 2 tablespoons (15 to 30 ml) vanilla extract

Pour the milk into the pressure cooking pot. Lock the lid in place. Select Yogurt and press Adjust until the display reads "boil." Turn the pressure release valve to the Sealed position. Alternatively, for pressure cookers that do not have the automatic boil function, use Slow Cook or Sauté to warm the milk to 185°F (85°C).

Remove the yogurt from the refrigerator and let it sit on the counter until ready to use.

When the boil cycle is complete and the milk reaches 185°F (85°C), about 1 hour, transfer the cooking pot to a wire rack to cool until the milk reaches 110°F (43°C), stirring occasionally. Transfer two to three ladlefuls of milk into a small bowl. Add the yogurt and whisk until smooth. Pour the starter mixture back into the cooking pot, whisking until well incorporated

Place the cooking pot back inside the pressure cooker. Lock the lid in place. Select Yogurt and press Adjust to incubate for 8 hours.

When the yogurt cycle is complete, place the pot of yogurt in the refrigerator to chill for 6 hours, or overnight. When chilled, divide the yogurt into two yogurt strainer bowls. Strain for 24 hours and then refrigerate. (In a pinch, you can also use nut milk bags or large coffee filters to strain.)

Transfer the strained yogurt to a bowl and add the honey and vanilla. Use a handheld electric mixer to whisk on medium speed until smooth. Place the yogurt in a large sealed container or three quart-size (946 ml) Mason jars and refrigerator for up to 2 weeks. Serve cold.

Top with your favorite flavors—Berry Cherry Chia Compote (page 132) or fresh fruit, honey, pure maple syrup, and granola. Layer the yogurt with the toppings for a fancy parfait.

YIELD: About 3 quarts (2.8 L)

TIP: Don't discard the whey! Use the whey as a buttermilk substitute in pancakes, waffles, muffins, or other baked goods. You can also use it in smoothies or in place of water in yeast bread.

BROWN SUGAR BANANA NUT BREAD

This moist and tender quick bread packs great banana flavor, and the brown sugar adds sweetness and color to the finished product.

1½ cups (188 g) all-purpose flour

1 teaspoon baking soda

½ teaspoon salt

¼ teaspoon ground cinnamon

1 cup (225 g) mashed very ripe banana (about 2 large bananas)

½ cup (115 g) packed light brown sugar

⅓ cup (80 ml) milk

¼ cup (60 ml) vegetable oil

2 large eggs

½ teaspoon vanilla extract

⅓ cup (40 g) chopped walnuts

Coat a half-size Bundt pan with nonstick cooking spray.

In a medium bowl, stir together the flour, baking soda, salt, and cinnamon. Set aside.

In a large bowl, whisk the banana, brown sugar, milk, vegetable oil, eggs, and vanilla until well blended. Add the dry ingredients and mix just until blended. Stir in the walnuts. Spoon the batter into the prepared Bundt pan. Cover the pan with a paper towel and cover the paper towel completely with aluminum foil, crimped around the edges to seal.

Pour 1 cup (235 ml) of water into the pressure cooking pot and place a trivet in the bottom. Carefully center the filled Bundt pan on a sling and lower the pan onto the trivet. Lock the lid in place and turn the pressure release valve to the Sealed position. Select High Pressure and 35 minutes cook time.

When the cook time ends, turn off the pressure cooker. Let the pressure release naturally for 5 minutes, and finish with a quick pressure release. When the valve drops, carefully remove the lid.

With the sling, transfer the pan to a wire rack. Remove the foil and paper towel. Cool, uncovered, for 5 minutes. Gently loosen the edges, remove the cake from the pan, and cool completely on a wire rack.

YIELD: 6 to 8 servings

► **TIP:** Before chopping, toast the walnuts in the pressure cooker on Browning/Sauté for about 2 minutes. Watch the nuts closely and stir frequently so they don't burn.

PINEAPPLE UPSIDE-DOWN BREAKFAST CAKE

Sweet, juicy pineapple and cherries make this a breakfast cake everyone will look forward to. Not only does it look pretty with a layer of pineapple slices on top, it's also a sweet treat that starts your day off with whole grains and protein.

Nonstick cooking spray, for preparing the pan

1 cup (120 g) whole-wheat pastry flour or (125 g) white whole-wheat flour

2 teaspoons baking powder

½ teaspoon salt

5 large eggs

½ cup (115 g) packed light brown sugar

2 tablespoons (28 g) unsalted butter, melted

1½ cups (345 g) plain Greek yogurt

1 teaspoon vanilla extract

1 cup (140 g) frozen cherries, thawed and halved

5 very thinly sliced fresh pineapple rings, cored (see Tip)

Spray a half-size Bundt pan with nonstick cooking spray.

In a medium bowl, whisk together the flour, baking powder, and salt. Set aside.

In a large bowl, whisk together the eggs and brown sugar until smooth. Add the butter, yogurt, and vanilla and continue whisking until smooth. Add the dry ingredients and mix just until blended. Fold in the cherries.

Place the pineapple slices in the bottom of the prepared Bundt pan. Spoon the batter on top of the pineapple.

Pour 1 cup (235 ml) of water into the pressure cooking pot and place a trivet in the bottom. Carefully center the filled pan on a sling and lower the pan into the cooking pot. Lock the lid in place and turn the pressure release valve to the Sealed position. Select High Pressure and 25 minutes cook time.

When the cook time ends, turn off the pressure cooker. Let the pressure release naturally for 10 minutes, and finish with a quick pressure release. When the valve drops, carefully remove the lid.

Use the sling to transfer the pan to a wire rack. Cool for 5 minutes. Gently loosen the edges, remove the cake from the pan, and cool completely on a wire rack. Serve warm.

YIELD: 4 to 6 servings

> **TIP:** Slicing the pineapple slices very thin allows them to form to the bottom of the Bundt pan, resulting in a prettier cake.

CARROT CAKE BREAKFAST CAKE WITH CREAM CHEESE YOGURT FROSTING

Carrot cake for breakfast!? Absolutely! This breakfast cake has all the flavors of a classic carrot cake—including the cream cheese frosting—and is a great way to start the day with whole grains and lots of protein.

Nonstick cooking spray, for preparing the pan

1 cup (120 g) whole-wheat pastry flour or (125 g) white whole-wheat flour

2 teaspoons baking powder

2 teaspoons ground cinnamon

½ teaspoon salt

½ teaspoon ground nutmeg

½ teaspoon ground ginger

5 large eggs

½ cup (115 g) packed light brown sugar

2 tablespoons (28 g) unsalted butter, melted

1½ cups (345 g) plain Greek yogurt

1 teaspoon vanilla extract

1½ cups (165 g) shredded carrots

¾ cup (110 g) raisins

Cream Cheese Yogurt Frosting (page 145)

Coat a half-size Bundt pan with nonstick cooking spray.

In a medium bowl, stir together the flour, baking powder, cinnamon, salt, nutmeg, and ginger. Set aside.

In a large bowl, whisk together the eggs and brown sugar until smooth. Add the butter, yogurt, and vanilla. Whisk again until smooth. Add the dry ingredients and whisk just until blended. Fold in the carrots and raisins. Spoon the batter into the prepared Bundt pan.

Pour 1 cup (235 ml) of water into the pressure cooking pot and place a trivet in the bottom. Carefully center the filled pan on a sling and lower the pan onto the trivet. Lock the lid in place and turn the pressure release valve to the Sealed position. Select High Pressure and 25 minutes cook time.

When the cook time ends, turn off the pressure cooker. Let the pressure release naturally for 10 minutes, and finish with a quick pressure release. When the valve drops, carefully remove the lid.

With the sling, transfer the pan to a wire rack to cool for 5 minutes. Gently loosen the edges, remove the cake from the pan, and cool 5 to 10 minutes on a wire rack. Serve warm with a drizzle of cream cheese yogurt frosting.

YIELD: 4 to 6 servings

> **TIP:** Save the leftovers! This cake reheats great—and it's also yummy eaten cold.

HONEY ORANGE POPPY SEED BREAKFAST CAKE WITH RASPBERRY-ORANGE SAUCE

This sweet orange poppy seed cake soaked in an orange juice and honey glaze and topped with a smooth, sweet raspberry sauce will make you feel like you're dining in a fancy breakfast cottage!

FOR BREAKFAST CAKE

Nonstick cooking spray, for preparing the pan

1 cup (120 g) whole-wheat pastry flour or (125 g) white whole-wheat flour

2 teaspoons baking powder

½ teaspoon salt

5 large eggs

¼ cup (50 g) sugar

2 tablespoons (28 g) unsalted butter, melted

1½ cups (345 g) plain Greek yogurt

1 teaspoon vanilla extract

Zest of 1 large orange

2 tablespoons (16 g) poppy seeds

FOR HONEY ORANGE GLAZE

¼ cup (60 ml) freshly squeezed orange juice

¼ cup (85 g) honey

Raspberry-Orange Yogurt Sauce (page 139)

To make the breakfast cake: Coat a half-size Bundt pan with nonstick cooking spray.

In a medium bowl, whisk the flour, baking powder, and salt. Set aside.

In a large bowl, whisk together the eggs and sugar until smooth. Add the butter, yogurt, vanilla, orange zest, and poppy seeds. Whisk again until smooth. Add the dry ingredients and whisk just until blended. Spoon the batter into the prepared Bundt pan.

Pour 1 cup (235 ml) of water into the pressure cooking pot and place a trivet in the bottom. Carefully center the filled pan on a sling and lower the pan onto the trivet. Lock the lid in place and turn the pressure release valve to the Sealed position. Select High Pressure and 25 minutes cook time.

While the cake cooks, make the honey orange glaze: In a small, microwave-safe bowl, whisk the orange juice and honey until well blended. Warm in the microwave on medium power until it combines easily when whisked, 10 to 20 seconds. Set aside.

When the cook time ends, turn off the pressure cooker. Let the pressure release naturally for 10 minutes, and finish with a quick pressure release. When the valve drops, carefully remove the lid. With the sling, transfer the pan to a wire rack.

Using a skewer, poke holes all over the cake. Pour the glaze over the top. Let cool 5 to 10 minutes, until the glaze soaks in. Gently loosen the edges, remove the cake from the pan, inverting it onto a plate to catch any remaining glaze. Serve warm with a scoop of Raspberry-Orange Yogurt Sauce drizzled over the top.

YIELD: 4 to 6 servings

► **TIP:** Swap the orange for lemon and top with fresh blueberries after baking for a delicious variation of the breakfast cake.

PUMPKIN-CHOCOLATE CHIP BREAKFAST CAKE

The popular flavor combo of pumpkin spice and chocolate means this delicious cake is the perfect choice for fall treats, or any time of year that pumpkin craving strikes!

Nonstick cooking spray, for preparing the pan

1 cup (120 g) whole-wheat pastry flour or (125 g) white whole-wheat flour

2 teaspoons baking powder

2 teaspoons ground cinnamon

1 teaspoon pumpkin pie spice

½ teaspoon salt

5 large eggs

½ cup (115 g) packed light brown sugar

2 tablespoons (28 g) unsalted butter, melted

¾ cup (180 g) plain Greek yogurt

¾ cup (185 g) pumpkin purée (solid-pack pumpkin)

1 teaspoon vanilla extract

½ cup (88 g) chocolate chips, milk or dark

Spray a half-size Bundt pan with nonstick cooking spray.

In a medium bowl, whisk together the flour, baking powder, cinnamon, pumpkin pie spice, and salt. Set aside.

In a large bowl, whisk together the eggs and brown sugar until smooth. Add the butter, yogurt, pumpkin, and vanilla and whisk until smooth. Add the dry ingredients and whisk just until blended. Fold in the chocolate chips. Spoon the batter into the prepared pan.

Pour 1 cup (235 ml) of water into the pressure cooking pot and place a trivet in the bottom. Carefully center the filled pan on a sling and lower the pan into the cooking pot. Lock the lid in place and turn the pressure release valve to the Sealed position. Select High Pressure and 25 minutes cook time.

When the cook time ends, turn off the pressure cooker. Let the pressure release naturally for 10 minutes, and finish with a quick pressure release. When the valve drops, carefully remove the lid.

Use the sling to transfer the pan to a wire rack. Cool for 5 minutes. Gently loosen the edges, remove the cake from the pan, and cool for 5 to 10 minutes on a wire rack. Serve warm.

YIELD: 4 to 6 servings

> **TIP:** If you like, omit the chocolate chips and, instead, serve with a drizzle of Dark Chocolate Syrup (page 136).

SWEET PEACH RASPBERRY SWIRL BREAKFAST CAKE

Peaches and raspberries are a taste match made in heaven! You'll fall in love at first bite with this sweet breakfast cake.

Nonstick cooking spray, for preparing the pan

1 cup (120 g) whole-wheat pastry flour or (125 g) white whole-wheat flour

2 teaspoons baking powder

½ teaspoon salt

5 large eggs

⅓ cup (67 g) sugar

2 tablespoons (28 g) unsalted butter, melted

1½ cups (345 g) plain Greek yogurt

1 teaspoon vanilla extract

1 cup (170 g) chopped peaches (fresh or bottled)

½ cup (160 g) seedless raspberry jam

Coat a half-size Bundt pan with nonstick cooking spray.

In a medium bowl, stir together the flour, baking powder, and salt.

In a large bowl, whisk together the eggs and sugar until smooth. Add the butter, yogurt, and vanilla. Whisk again until smooth. Add the dry ingredients and whisk just until blended.

Fold in the peaches. Spoon the batter into the prepared Bundt pan.

In a small bowl, warm the raspberry jam in the microwave on medium power just until it's loose enough to stir. Drizzle the warm jam over the batter. With a knife, swirl the jam throughout the cake.

Pour 1 cup (235 ml) of water into the pressure cooking pot and place a trivet in the bottom. Carefully center the filled pan on a sling and lower the pan onto the trivet. Lock the lid in place and turn the pressure release valve to the Sealed position. Select High Pressure and 30 minutes cook time.

When the cook time ends, turn off the pressure cooker. Let the pressure release naturally for 10 minutes, and finish with a quick pressure release. When the valve drops, carefully remove the lid.

With the sling, transfer the pan to a wire rack. Cool, for 5 minutes. Gently loosen the edges, remove the cake from the pan, and cool for 5 to 10 minutes on the wire rack. Serve warm.

YIELD: 4 to 6 servings

> **TIP:** For an extra-special treat, drizzle the warm cake with Cream Cheese Yogurt Frosting (page 145).

OVERNIGHT CINNAMON-PECAN MONKEY BREAD

Monkey bread is also known as "bubble bread" or "pull-apart bread." This easy overnight version starts with frozen dinner rolls, so it rises overnight in the refrigerator and is quick and easy to "bake" in the pressure cooker in the morning.

FOR MONKEY BREAD

16 frozen unbaked white yeast dinner rolls (see Tip)

Nonstick cooking spray, for preparing the pan

⅓ cup (75 g) packed light brown sugar

1½ teaspoons ground cinnamon

¼ cup (28 g) pecans, finely chopped and toasted

¼ cup (55 g) unsalted butter

FOR GLAZE

½ cup (60 g) powdered sugar

2 teaspoons milk

To make the monkey bread: The night before, place the frozen rolls in a zip-top bag and thaw at room temperature for 60 to 90 minutes. Do not let rise. When thawed, cut each roll in half.

Coat a half-size Bundt pan with nonstick cooking spray.

In a small bowl, stir together the brown sugar, cinnamon, and pecans. In a second small bowl, melt the butter in the microwave. Dip the roll halves in the butter and then roll them in the brown sugar mixture until coated. Place the rolls in the prepared Bundt pan, staggering the dough balls to build layers. Cover the Bundt pan with aluminum foil and refrigerate overnight.

In the morning, remove the Bundt pan from the refrigerator. Pour 1 cup (235 ml) of water into the pressure cooking pot and place a trivet in the bottom. Carefully center the filled pan on a sling and lower the pan onto the trivet. Lock the lid in place and turn the pressure release valve to the Sealed position. Select High Pressure and 25 minutes cook time.

When the cook time ends, turn off the pressure cooker. Let the pressure release naturally for 5 minutes, and finish with a quick pressure release. When the valve drops, carefully remove the lid.

With the sling, transfer the pan to a wire rack. Invert the bread onto a serving plate.

To make the glaze: In a small bowl, whisk the powdered sugar and milk until smooth. Drizzle the glaze over the top and sides of the bread. Serve warm.

YIELD: 8 servings

> **TIP:** The roll dough used in this recipe is the kind you thaw, rise, and bake, not the partially baked rolls.

Cheesecakes

Cheesecakes seem to be the thing that new cooks are most excited to make in their new pressure cookers. Who can blame them? The pressure cooker is the perfect environment for "baking" cheesecake, and pressure cooker cheesecakes are oh so rich, smooth, and creamy.

▶ Classic Cherry Cheesecake	40
▶ Tropical Cheesecake	41
▶ Strawberry Swirl Cheesecake with White Chocolate Ganache	42
▶ Vanilla Confetti Cheesecake	44
▶ Pumpkin Vanilla Layered Cheesecake with Maple Glaze	46
▶ Red Velvet Cheesecake with Vanilla Yogurt Glaze	48
▶ Triple Layer Chocolate Mint Cheesecake	50
▶ Caramel Pecan Cheesecake	52
▶ Japanese Cheesecake	54
▶ Oreo-Chocolate Chip Mini Cheesecakes	55
▶ Key Lime Cheesecake	56
▶ Mini Lemon Cheesecakes in a Jar	57

◀ Vanilla Confetti Cheesecake, page 44

CLASSIC CHERRY CHEESECAKE

You can't go wrong with a classic cheesecake! This cheesecake is so rich, smooth, and creamy, your family will ask you to make it all the time.

FOR CRUST

Nonstick cooking spray, for preparing the pan

1 cup (60 g) graham cracker crumbs (about 8 crackers, crushed)

3 tablespoons (42 g) unsalted butter, melted

1 tablespoon (13 g) sugar

FOR FILLING

2 packages (8 ounces, or 225 g, each) cream cheese, at room temperature

½ cup (100 g) sugar

¼ cup (60 g) sour cream

1 tablespoon (8 g) all-purpose flour

1 teaspoon vanilla extract

2 large eggs, at room temperature

Cherry Pie Filling (page 150), for serving

To make the crust: Coat a 7-inch (18 cm) springform pan with nonstick cooking spray.

In a small bowl, stir together the graham cracker crumbs, butter, and sugar. Spread the crust evenly in the bottom and no more than 1 inch (2.5 cm) up the side of the prepared pan. Freeze for 10 minutes.

To make the filling: In a large bowl, with a handheld electric mixer, mix the cream cheese and sugar on medium speed until smooth. Blend in the sour cream, flour, and vanilla. One at a time, add the eggs and mix just until blended. Do not overmix. Pour the batter over the crust.

Pour 1 cup (235 ml) of water into the pressure cooking pot and place a trivet in the bottom. Carefully center the filled pan on a sling and lower the pan onto the trivet. Lock the lid in place and turn the pressure release valve to the Sealed position. Select High Pressure and 25 minutes cook time.

When the cook time ends, turn off the pressure cooker. Let the pressure release naturally for 10 minutes, and finish with a quick pressure release. When the valve drops, carefully remove the lid. Use an instant-read thermometer to check that the cheesecake has reached 150°F (65.5°C) in the center. If not, relock the lid and cook the cheesecake at High Pressure for 5 minutes more, followed by another 10-minute natural pressure release.

With the sling, transfer the pan to a wire rack to cool. Soak up any water that may have collected on top of the cheesecake with the corner of a paper towel.

When the cheesecake is cool, refrigerate, covered with plastic wrap, for at least 4 hours, or overnight, until ready to serve.

Serve topped with Cherry Pie Filling.

YIELD: 6 to 8 servings

▶ **TIP:** Some people like to cook cheesecake covered with aluminum foil to avoid getting droplets of water on the top; if you prefer this method, add at least 5 minutes to the cook time.

CHANGE IT UP!

This recipe is so versatile, you'll want to make it often using different toppings. The Triple Berry (page 155) and Strawberry Pie Fillings (page 154) are great with this recipe.

- ▸ PREP TIME: 15 minutes
- ▸ COOK TIME: 25 minutes
- ▸ TOTAL TIME: 1 hour, 10 minutes, plus chilling time

TROPICAL CHEESECAKE

A rich, coconut cheesecake with a coconut cookie crust topped with sweet pineapple. Enjoy a taste of the tropics in every bite!

FOR CRUST

Nonstick cooking spray, for preparing the pan

1 cup (142 g) coconut cookie crumbs (about 12 cookies, crushed)

2 tablespoons (28 g) unsalted butter, melted

FOR FILLING

2 packages (8 ounces, or 225 g, each) cream cheese, at room temperature

⅓ cup (67 g) sugar

⅓ cup (80 ml) cream of coconut (see Tip)

1 tablespoon (8 g) all-purpose flour

½ teaspoon vanilla extract

2 large eggs, at room temperature

FOR SERVING

Pineapple Sauce (page 140)

Maraschino cherries, for garnishing (optional)

To make the crust: Coat a 7-inch (18 cm) springform pan with nonstick cooking spray.

In a small bowl, stir together the cookie crumbs and butter. Spread the crust evenly in the bottom and no more than 1 inch (2.5 cm) up the side of the prepared pan. Freeze for 10 minutes.

To make the filling: In a large bowl, with a handheld electric mixer, mix the cream cheese and sugar on medium speed until smooth. Blend in the cream of coconut, flour, and vanilla. One at a time, add the eggs and mix just until blended. Do not overmix. Pour the batter over the crust.

Pour 1 cup (235 ml) of water into the pressure cooking pot and place a trivet in the bottom. Carefully center the filled pan on a sling and lower the pan onto the trivet. Lock the lid in place and turn the pressure release valve to the Sealed position. Select High Pressure and 25 minutes cook time.

When the cook time ends, turn off the pressure cooker. Let the pressure release naturally for 10 minutes, and finish with a quick pressure release. When the valve drops, carefully remove the lid. Use an instant-read thermometer to check that the cheesecake has reached 150°F (65.5°C) in the center. If not, relock the lid and cook the cheesecake at High Pressure for 5 minutes more, followed by another 10-minute natural pressure release.

With the sling, transfer the pan to a wire rack to cool. Soak up any water that may have collected on top of the cheesecake with the corner of a paper towel.

When the cheesecake is cool, refrigerate, covered with plastic wrap, for at least 4 hours, or overnight, until ready to serve.

Serve topped with Pineapple Sauce and a maraschino cherry, if desired.

YIELD: 6 to 8 servings

▸ **TIP:** Cream of coconut is used to make tropical drinks such as piña coladas. You'll find it in the drink aisle.

CHANGE IT UP!
If you're not a fan of pineapple, try this coconut cheesecake drizzled with Chocolate Ganache (page 139).

STRAWBERRY SWIRL CHEESECAKE WITH WHITE CHOCOLATE GANACHE

A sweet strawberry swirl throughout and a rich white chocolate ganache over the top really makes this cheesecake shine!

FOR CRUST

Nonstick cooking spray, for preparing the pan

1 cup (142 g) Oreo cookie crumbs (about 12 cookies, crushed)

2 tablespoons (28 g) unsalted butter, melted

FOR FILLING

2 packages (8 ounces, or 225 g, each) cream cheese, at room temperature

½ cup (100 g) sugar

½ cup (115 g) plain Greek yogurt

2 tablespoons (16 g) all-purpose flour

2 teaspoons vanilla extract

3 large eggs, at room temperature

¼ cup (80 g) seedless strawberry jam or jelly

FOR WHITE CHOCOLATE GANACHE

6 ounces (170 g) white chocolate, finely chopped

⅓ cup (80 ml) heavy cream

FOR SERVING

Fresh strawberries, sliced (optional)

To make the crust: Coat a 7-inch (18 cm) springform pan with nonstick cooking spray.

In a small bowl, stir together the cookie crumbs and butter. Spread the crust evenly in the bottom and no more than 1 inch (2.5 cm) up the side of the prepared pan. Freeze for 10 minutes.

To make the filling: In a large bowl, with a handheld electric mixer, mix the cream cheese and sugar on medium speed until smooth. Blend in the yogurt, flour, and vanilla. One at a time, add the eggs and mix just until blended. Do not overmix. Pour half the batter over the crust.

In a small, microwave-safe bowl, warm the strawberry jam in the microwave on high power until it's loose, about 10 seconds. Spoon dollops of jam on top of the batter and use a knife to swirl the jam through the batter. (Be careful to avoid mixing the jam into the batter—four or five swirls with the knife are all you need.) Pour the remaining batter over the swirled jam layer.

Pour 1 cup (235 ml) of water into the pressure cooking pot and place a trivet in the bottom. Carefully center the filled pan on a sling and lower the pan onto the trivet. Lock the lid in place and turn the pressure release valve to the Sealed position. Select High Pressure and 40 minutes cook time.

When the cook time ends, turn off the pressure cooker. Let the pressure release naturally for 10 minutes, and finish with a quick pressure release. When the valve drops, carefully remove the lid. Use an instant-read thermometer to check that the cheesecake has reached 150°F (65.5°C) in the center. If not, relock the lid and cook the cheesecake at High Pressure for 5 minutes more, followed by another 10-minute natural pressure release.

CHANGE IT UP!
Use raspberry jam and a graham cracker crust for a delicious variation of this cheesecake.

With the sling, transfer the pan to a wire rack to cool. Soak up any water that may have collected on top of the cheesecake with the corner of a paper towel.

When the cheesecake is cool, refrigerate, covered with plastic wrap, for at least 4 hours, or overnight.

To make the white chocolate ganache: Place the white chocolate in a small bowl. In a small saucepan over medium heat, stirring lightly, bring the cream just to a simmer with bubbles barely forming around the edges of the pan. Immediately remove from the heat and pour the warmed cream over the white chocolate. Cover the bowl and let sit for 5 minutes to melt the chocolate. Whisk until smooth. Let the ganache cool for 10 minutes at room temperature. Pour it over the chilled cheesecake, letting it drizzle down the sides. Refrigerate until ready to serve. Garnish with sliced strawberries right before serving, if desired.

YIELD: 6 to 8 servings

▸ PREP TIME: 20 minutes

▸ COOK TIME: 35 minutes

▸ TOTAL TIME: 1 hour,
15 minutes,
plus chilling time

VANILLA CONFETTI CHEESECAKE

This colorful cheesecake will delight children and adults alike! Perfect for birthdays or any time you're celebrating.

FOR CRUST

Nonstick cooking spray, for preparing the pan

1½ cups (213 g) Golden Oreo crumbs (about 18 cookies, crushed)

3 tablespoons (42 g) unsalted butter, melted

FOR FILLING

2 packages (8 ounces, or 225 g, each) cream cheese, at room temperature

½ cup (100 g) sugar

¼ cup (60 g) plain Greek yogurt (see Tip opposite)

½ cup (54 g) boxed yellow cake mix

2 teaspoons vanilla extract

2 large eggs, at room temperature

¼ cup (40 g) sprinkles, plus more for garnishing

FOR SERVING

Vanilla Whipped Cream (page 148)

To make the crust: Coat a 7-inch (18 cm) springform pan with nonstick cooking spray.

In a small bowl, stir together the cookie crumbs and butter. Spread the crust evenly in the bottom and no more than 1 inch (2.5 cm) up the side of the prepared pan. Freeze for 10 minutes.

To make the filling: In a large bowl, with a handheld electric mixer, mix the cream cheese and sugar on medium speed until smooth. Blend in the yogurt, cake mix, and vanilla. One at a time, add the eggs and mix just until blended. Do not overmix. Working quickly so the color on the sprinkles doesn't run, stir in the sprinkles and pour the batter over the crust.

Pour 1 cup (235 ml) of water into the pressure cooking pot and place a trivet in the bottom. Carefully center the filled pan on a sling and lower the pan onto the trivet. Lock the lid in place and turn the pressure release valve to the Sealed position. Select High Pressure and 35 minutes cook time.

When the cook time ends, turn off the pressure cooker. Let the pressure release naturally for 10 minutes, and finish with a quick pressure release. When the valve drops, carefully remove the lid. Use an instant-read thermometer to check that the cheesecake has reached 150°F (65.5°C) in the center. If not, relock the lid and cook the cheesecake at High Pressure for 5 minutes more, followed by another 10-minute natural pressure release.

CHANGE IT UP!
Make a fun cupcake-style version of this cheesecake by preparing the filling as directed and then following the directions for the Mini Lemon Cheesecakes in a Jar (page 57) to cook them in individual Mason jars. Use a large or jumbo piping tip to pipe on Vanilla Whipped Cream (page 148) and garnish with sprinkles.

With the sling, transfer the pan to a wire rack to cool. Soak up any water that may have collected on top of the cheesecake with the corner of a paper towel.

When the cheesecake is cool, refrigerate, covered with plastic wrap, for at least 4 hours, or overnight, until ready to serve.

Just prior to serving, spread or pipe the whipped cream on top of the cheesecake. Garnish with a few more sprinkles.

YIELD: 6 to 8 servings

> **TIP:** Be sure to use Greek yogurt that's either full fat or 2 percent fat—the fat-free varieties can make your cheesecake batter thinner than it should be.

PUMPKIN VANILLA LAYERED CHEESECAKE WITH MAPLE GLAZE

Pumpkin spices pair perfectly with ginger, vanilla, and maple to make this cheesecake an explosion of cozy flavors. This is the perfect elegant fall dessert!

FOR CRUST

Nonstick cooking spray, for preparing the pan

1½ cups (95 g) gingersnap cookie crumbs

3 tablespoons (42 g) unsalted butter, melted

FOR FILLING

2 packages (8 ounces, or 225 g, each) cream cheese, at room temperature

½ cup (115 g) packed light brown sugar

¼ cup (60 g) plain Greek yogurt

2 tablespoons (16 g) all-purpose flour

1 teaspoon vanilla extract

2 large eggs, at room temperature

½ cup (123 g) pumpkin purée (solid-pack pumpkin)

2 teaspoons pumpkin pie spice

FOR MAPLE GLAZE

2 tablespoons (28 g) unsalted butter

¼ cup (60 ml) pure maple syrup

½ cup (60 g) powdered sugar

⅛ teaspoon maple extract (optional)

To make the crust: Coat a 7-inch (18 cm) springform pan with nonstick cooking spray.

In a small bowl, stir together the gingersnap crumbs and butter. Spread the crust evenly in the bottom and no more than 1 inch (2.5 cm) up the side of the prepared pan. Freeze for 10 minutes.

To make the filling: In a large bowl, with a handheld electric mixer, mix the cream cheese and brown sugar on medium speed until smooth. Blend in the yogurt, flour, and vanilla. One at a time, add the eggs and mix just until blended. Do not overmix. Pour 1 cup (240 g) of batter over the crust.

To the remaining batter, with a spatula, stir in the pumpkin purée and pumpkin pie spice just until combined. Pour the pumpkin batter into the pan, starting near the edges of the pan and pouring toward the center. Smooth the top with a spoon or offset spatula.

Pour 1 cup (235 ml) of water into the pressure cooking pot and place a trivet in the bottom. Carefully center the filled pan on a sling and lower the pan onto the trivet. Lock the lid in place and turn the pressure release valve to the Sealed position. Select High Pressure and 35 minutes cook time.

When the cook time ends, turn off the pressure cooker. Let the pressure release naturally for 10 minutes, and finish with a quick pressure release. When the valve drops, carefully remove the lid. Use an instant-read thermometer to check that the cheesecake has reached 150°F (65.5°C) in the center. If not, relock the lid and cook the cheesecake at High Pressure for 5 minutes more, followed by another 10-minute natural pressure release.

CHANGE IT UP!
Use Oreo cookie crumbs
for the crust and replace
the maple glaze with
Chocolate Ganache
(page 139) for a
pumpkin-chocolate
flavor combination.

With the sling, transfer the pan to
a wire rack to cool. Soak up any
water that may have collected on
top of the cheesecake with the
corner of a paper towel.

When the cheesecake is cool,
cover with plastic wrap and
refrigerate for at least 4 hours,
or overnight.

To make the maple glaze: In a
small saucepan over medium
heat, melt the butter. Add the
maple syrup, powdered sugar,
and maple extract. Whisk until
smooth. Let cool for 10 minutes.
Whisk again, and slowly pour the
glaze over the chilled cheesecake, letting it drizzle down the
sides. Refrigerate until ready
to serve.

YIELD: 6 to 8 servings

➤ **TIP:** When layering cheesecake batter, always pour from
the outside of the pan toward the center. This helps keep
an evenly layered look.

RED VELVET CHEESECAKE WITH VANILLA YOGURT GLAZE

Red velvet cheesecake is as beloved as it is beautiful. This version features the hallmark rich chocolate flavor and bright red color.

FOR CRUST

Nonstick cooking spray, for preparing the pan

1 cup (142 g) Oreo cookie crumbs (about 12 cookies, crushed)

2 tablespoons (28 g) unsalted butter, melted

FOR FILLING

1 cup (175 g) milk chocolate chips

2 packages (8 ounces, or 225 g, each) cream cheese, at room temperature

⅓ cup (67 g) sugar

¼ cup (60 g) plain Greek yogurt

1 tablespoon (8 g) cornstarch

1 teaspoon red food coloring

1 teaspoon vanilla extract

2 large eggs, at room temperature

FOR VANILLA YOGURT GLAZE

1 cup (240 g) plain or vanilla yogurt

2 tablespoons (16 g) powdered sugar

½ teaspoon vanilla extract

Chocolate curls, for garnishing (optional)

To make the crust: Coat a 7-inch (18 cm) springform pan with nonstick cooking spray.

In a small bowl, stir together the cookie crumbs and butter. Spread the crust evenly in the bottom and no more than 1 inch (2.5 cm) up the side of the prepared pan. Freeze for 10 minutes.

To make the filling: In a small microwave-safe bowl, melt the milk chocolate chips in the microwave on medium power for 1 minute. Stir. If not completely melted, microwave for another 30 seconds. Set aside to cool.

In a large bowl, with a handheld electric mixer, mix the cream cheese and sugar on medium speed until smooth. Blend in the yogurt, cornstarch, red food coloring, and vanilla. One at a time, add the eggs. While gently stirring, pour in the melted chocolate and mix just until blended. Do not overmix. Pour the batter over the crust.

Pour 1 cup (235 ml) of water into the pressure cooking pot and place a trivet in the bottom. Carefully center the filled pan on a sling and lower the pan onto the trivet. Lock the lid in place and turn the pressure release valve to the Sealed position. Select High Pressure and 35 minutes cook time.

When the cook time ends, turn off the pressure cooker. Let the pressure release naturally for 10 minutes, and finish with a quick pressure release. When the valve drops, carefully remove the lid. Use an instant-read thermometer to check that the cheesecake has reached 150°F (65.5°C) in the center. If not, relock the lid and cook the cheesecake at High Pressure for 5 minutes more, followed by another 10-minute natural pressure release.

CHANGE IT UP!
Make this rich dessert even sweeter: Top it with **White Chocolate Ganache** (see subrecipe on page 42).

With the sling, transfer the pan to a wire rack to cool. Soak up any water that may have collected on top of the cheesecake with the corner of a paper towel.

When the cheesecake is cool, cover with plastic wrap and refrigerate for at least 4 hours, or overnight.

To make the Vanilla Yogurt Glaze: In a small bowl, whisk the yogurt, powdered sugar, and vanilla to combine. Spoon the glaze over the cheesecake and smooth it out to the edges. Garnish with chocolate curls, if desired. Refrigerate until ready to serve.

YIELD: 6 to 8 servings

▶ **TIP:** For a more intense red color, use red no-taste gel. You can find this concentrated food coloring at many local big-box stores and any store that sells specialty baking supplies.

TRIPLE LAYER CHOCOLATE MINT CHEESECAKE

A refreshing mint layer is complemented by white and dark chocolate layers in this beautiful triple-layered cake. It's simple to make but impressive to serve.

FOR CRUST

Nonstick cooking spray, for preparing the pan

1 cup (142 g) Mint Oreo cookie crumbs (about 12 cookies, crushed)

2 tablespoons (28 g) unsalted butter, melted

FOR FILLING

2 packages (8 ounces, or 225 g, each) cream cheese, at room temperature

½ cup (100 g) sugar

¼ cup (60 g) plain Greek yogurt

1 tablespoon (8 g) cornstarch

1 teaspoon vanilla extract

2 large eggs, at room temperature

2 ounces (60 g) semisweet chocolate

4 ounces (120 g) white chocolate, divided

1 teaspoon mint extract

3 drops green food coloring

FOR SERVING

Vanilla Yogurt Glaze (page 48; optional)

To make the crust: Coat a 7-inch (18 cm) springform pan with nonstick cooking spray.

In a small bowl, stir together the cookie crumbs and butter. Spread the crust evenly in the bottom and no more than 1 inch (2.5 cm) up the side of the prepared pan. Freeze for 10 minutes.

To make the filling: In a large bowl, with a handheld electric mixer, mix the cream cheese and sugar on medium speed until smooth. Blend in the yogurt, cornstarch, and vanilla. One at a time, add the eggs and mix just until blended. Do not overmix. Equally divide the batter among three small bowls and set aside.

In a small microwave-safe bowl, melt the semisweet chocolate in the microwave at medium power for 30 seconds. Stir. Continue to microwave until the chocolate is completely melted and smooth, another 15 to 30 seconds. Stir. Whisk the melted chocolate into the first bowl of batter until completely combined. Pour onto the crust and smooth the top.

Using the same process, in another small bowl, melt 2 ounces (60 g) of white chocolate. Whisk the white chocolate into the second bowl of cheesecake batter. Starting at the edge of the pan and moving toward the center, gently pour the white chocolate layer over the chocolate layer. Smooth the top.

In a third small bowl, melt the remaining 2 ounces (60 g) of white chocolate. Whisk into the last bowl of batter. Add the mint extract and food coloring and stir until completely incorporated. Gently pour the mint layer over the white chocolate layer, again from the edge toward the middle. Smooth the top.

Pour 1 cup (235 ml) of water into the pressure cooking pot and place a trivet in the bottom. Carefully center the filled pan on a sling and lower the pan onto the trivet. Lock the lid in place and turn the pressure release valve to the Sealed position. Select High Pressure and 35 minutes cook time.

CHANGE IT UP!
You can easily transform this into a chocolate orange cheesecake by swapping out the mint extract for orange extract and using lemon- or chocolate-flavored Oreo cookies for the crust.

When the cook time ends, turn off the pressure cooker. Let the pressure release naturally for 10 minutes, and finish with a quick pressure release. When the valve drops, carefully remove the lid. Use an instant-read thermometer to check that the cheesecake has reached 150°F (65.5°C) in the center. If not, relock the lid and cook the cheesecake at High Pressure for 5 minutes more, followed by another 10-minute natural pressure release.

With the sling, transfer the pan to a wire rack to cool. Soak up any water that may have collected on top of the cheesecake with the corner of a paper towel.

When the cheesecake is cool, cover with plastic wrap and refrigerate at least 4 hours, or overnight. Prior to serving, top the chilled cheesecake with the Vanilla Yogurt Glaze, if desired. Refrigerate until ready to serve.

YIELD: 6 to 8 servings

▶ **TIP:** To make pretty chocolate garnishes, melt some chocolate until smooth and pour it into a zip-top bag or piping bag. Clip a very small hole in a bottom corner of the bag. Draw designs on a piece of parchment paper. Place in the freezer to harden and transfer to the top of the cake.

CARAMEL PECAN CHEESECAKE

Indulge in this creamy, smooth filling sweetened with brown sugar on a shortbread pecan crust with a decadent caramel topping studded with toasted pecans.

FOR CRUST

Nonstick cooking spray, for preparing the pan

¾ cup (140 g) crushed Pecan Sandies cookies (about 9 cookies)

¼ cup (28 g) toasted pecans, finely chopped

2 tablespoons (28 g) unsalted butter, melted

FOR FILLING

2 packages (8 ounces, or 225 g, each) cream cheese, at room temperature

½ cup (115 g) packed light brown sugar

¼ cup (60 ml) heavy cream

1 tablespoon (8 g) all-purpose flour

½ teaspoon vanilla extract

2 large eggs, at room temperature

FOR CARAMEL PECAN TOPPING

½ cup (120 g) caramel ice cream topping or Dulce de Leche (page 146)

½ cup (56 g) toasted pecans

To make the crust: Coat a 7-inch (18 cm) springform pan with nonstick cooking spray.

In a small bowl, stir together the cookie crumbs, pecans, and butter. Spread the crust evenly in the bottom and no more than 1 inch (2.5 cm) up the side of the prepared pan. Freeze for 10 minutes.

To make the filling: In a large bowl, with a handheld electric mixer, mix the cream cheese and brown sugar on medium speed until smooth. Blend in the cream, flour, and vanilla. One at a time, add the eggs and mix just until blended. Do not overmix. Pour the batter over the crust.

Pour 1 cup (235 ml) of water into the pressure cooking pot and place a trivet in the bottom. Carefully center the filled pan on a sling and lower the pan onto the trivet. Lock the lid in place and turn the pressure release valve to the Sealed position. Select High Pressure and 25 minutes cook time.

When the cook time ends, turn off the pressure cooker. Let the pressure release naturally for 10 minutes, and finish with a quick pressure release. When the valve drops, carefully remove the lid. Use an instant-read thermometer to check that the cheesecake has reached 150°F (65.5°C) in the center. If not, relock the lid and cook the cheesecake at High Pressure for 5 minutes more, followed by another 10-minute natural pressure release.

With the sling, transfer the pan to a wire rack to cool. Soak up any water that may have collected on top of the cheesecake with the corner of a paper towel.

When the cheesecake is cool, cover with plastic wrap and refrigerate for at least 4 hours, or overnight, until ready to serve.

To make the Caramel Pecan Topping: Just before serving, in a small bowl, stir together the caramel sauce and pecans. Spread over the cheesecake.

YIELD: 6 to 8 servings

▸ **TIP:** Adding the caramel topping to the uncut cheesecake makes for a pretty presentation, but it's easier to slice and eat if you top individual slices instead.

▶ PREP TIME: 15 minutes

▶ COOK TIME: 20 minutes

▶ TOTAL TIME: 55 minutes

JAPANESE CHEESECAKE

Lighter and less sweet than traditional cheesecake, Japanese cheesecake is sort of a cross between cheesecake and angel food cake. This cheesecake has a mild lemon flavor and can be served warm or cold. A great option when you don't have time for an overnight chill.

Nonstick cooking spray, for preparing the pan

4 ounces (115 g) cream cheese, cubed

⅓ cup (80 ml) whole milk

3 tablespoons (42 g) unsalted butter

4 large eggs, separated

⅛ teaspoon cream of tartar

⅛ teaspoon salt

⅔ cup (67 g) sugar

1 tablespoon (15 g) freshly squeezed lemon juice

1 teaspoon vanilla extract

⅓ cup (42 g) all-purpose flour

2 tablespoons (16 g) cornstarch

Powdered sugar, for decorating

Fresh berries, for serving

Coat a 7-inch (18 cm) springform pan with nonstick cooking spray. Line the bottom of the pan with a parchment paper round and the side with a parchment strip cut to be 1-inch (2.5 cm) higher than the pan's edge.

In a small saucepan over medium heat, combine the cream cheese, milk, and butter. Cook, whisking occasionally, until smooth. Remove from the heat and cool slightly, about 5 minutes.

In a large bowl, using a handheld electric mixer, beat the egg whites, cream of tartar, and salt on medium speed until soft peaks form, about 3 minutes. Gradually add the sugar and continue beating until stiff peaks form, about 3 minutes longer.

In a medium bowl, beat the egg yolks, lemon juice, and vanilla on medium speed until smooth. Pour the cooled cream cheese mixture into the yolk mixture and beat until smooth. Add the flour and cornstarch and mix on low speed just until blended. Using a large spoon, stir in half the beaten egg whites just until combined. Fold in the remaining beaten egg whites. Pour into the prepared pan.

Pour 1 cup (235 ml) of water into the pressure cooking pot and place a trivet in the bottom. Use a sling to lower the pan into the cooking pot. Lock the lid in place and turn the pressure release valve to the Sealed position. Select High Pressure and 20 minutes cook time.

When complete, turn off the pressure cooker. Let the pressure release naturally for 10 minutes, and finish with a quick pressure release. When the valve drops, carefully remove the lid.

Use the sling to transfer the pan to a wire rack. Blot the top of the cheesecake with a paper towel to absorb any water. After cooling 10 minutes, transfer the cake to a serving plate, sprinkle with powdered sugar, and serve warm with fresh berries. Or refrigerate until ready to serve.

YIELD: 6 to 8 servings

▶ **TIP:** It's very important that no egg yolk gets into the egg whites. Crack the eggs one at a time and separate the whites into a small bowl. Pour the contents into a larger bowl when you are sure they have no yolk in the whites.

- ▸ PREP TIME: 5 minutes
- ▸ COOK TIME: 3 minutes
- ▸ TOTAL TIME: 4 hours, or overnight

OREO-CHOCOLATE CHIP MINI CHEESECAKES

Mini cheesecakes are easy to make, come together in a snap, and are perfectly portion controlled. Instead of putting a crust on the bottom, we made the recipe even easier by putting an Oreo cookie on top.

Nonstick cooking spray, for preparing the custard cups

1 package (8 ounces, or 225 g) cream cheese, at room temperature

¼ cup (50 g) sugar

2 tablespoons (30 g) sour cream

½ teaspoon vanilla extract

Pinch salt

1 large egg, at room temperature

½ cup (90 g) mini chocolate chips

Vanilla Whipped Cream (page 118), for serving (optional)

Oreo cookies, for serving (optional)

Coat six (6-ounce, or 180 ml) glass custard cups with nonstick cooking spray.

In a large bowl, with a handheld electric mixer, mix the cream cheese and sugar on medium speed until smooth. Blend in the sour cream, vanilla, and salt. Mix in the egg just until blended. Do not overmix. Gently stir in the mini chocolate chips. Equally divide the batter among the prepared cups. (The cups will be about halfway full because the cheesecakes need room to rise as they cook.)

Pour 1 cup (235 ml) of water into the pressure cooking pot and place a trivet in the bottom. Carefully place three cups on the trivet. Place a second trivet on top of the cups and place the remaining three cups on top. Lock the lid in place and turn the pressure release valve to the Sealed position. Select High Pressure and 3 minutes cook time.

When the cook time ends, turn off the pressure cooker. Let the pressure release naturally for 10 minutes, and finish with a quick pressure release. When the valve drops, carefully remove the lid.

Transfer the cups to a wire rack to cool. Soak up any water that may have collected on top of the cheesecakes with the corner of a paper towel. When the cheesecakes are cool, cover with plastic wrap and refrigerate for at least 4 hours, or overnight.

Decorate each cheesecake with whipped cream and a whole Oreo, if desired.

YIELD: 6 servings

> ▸ **TIP:** Always use a trivet when cooking pot in pot to avoid cooking directly on the heating element.

- ▸ PREP TIME: 15 minutes
- ▸ COOK TIME: 25 minutes
- ▸ TOTAL TIME: 4 hours or overnight

KEY LIME CHEESECAKE

When you can't decide, try this recipe, which is a cross between key lime pie and cheesecake. It has a tart lime flavor like key lime pie, but it's richer and creamier, like a cheesecake.

FOR CRUST

Nonstick cooking spray, for preparing the pan

1 cup (60 g) graham cracker crumbs (about 8 crackers, crushed)

3 tablespoons (42 g) unsalted butter, melted

1 tablespoon (13 g) sugar

FOR FILLING

1 package (8 ounces, or 225 g) cream cheese, at room temperature

1 can (14 ounces, or 425 ml) sweetened condensed milk

⅓ cup (80 ml) freshly squeezed key lime juice (see Tip)

1 large egg

1 tablespoon (6 g) grated key lime zest

Vanilla Whipped Cream (page 148), for serving

Thin lime slices, for serving

To make the crust: Coat a 7-inch (18 cm) springform pan with nonstick cooking spray.

In a small bowl, stir together the graham cracker crumbs, butter, and sugar. Spread the crust evenly in the bottom and no more than 1 inch (2.5 cm) up the side of the pan. Freeze for 10 minutes.

To make the filling: In a large bowl, using a handheld electric mixer, beat the cream cheese on medium speed until smooth. Gradually blend in the sweetened condensed milk. Beat in the key lime juice. Mix in the egg just until blended; don't over mix. Stir in the key lime zest. Pour the batter into the prepared pan.

Pour 1 cup (235 ml) of water into the pressure cooking pot and place a trivet in the bottom. Carefully center the filled pan on a sling and lower the pan into the cooking pot. Lock the lid in place and turn the pressure release valve to the Sealed position. Select High Pressure and 25 minutes cook time.

When the cook time ends, turn off the pressure cooker. Let the pressure release naturally for 10 minutes, and finish with a quick pressure release. When the valve drops, carefully remove the lid. Use an instant-read thermometer to check that the cheesecake has reached 150°F (65.5°C) in the center. If not, relock the lid and cook the cheesecake at High Pressure for 5 minutes more, followed by another 10-minute natural pressure release.

Use the sling to transfer the pan to a wire rack to cool. Soak up any water that may have collected on top of the cheesecake with the corner of a paper towel.

Once the cheesecake is cool, cover with plastic wrap and refrigerate for at least 4 hours, or overnight, until ready to serve.

Serve topped with Vanilla Whipped Cream and thinly sliced lime slices.

YIELD: 6 to 8 servings

▸ **TIP:** If you can't find key limes, substitute 3 tablespoons (45 ml) freshly squeezed lime juice and 2 tablespoons (30 ml) freshly squeezed lemon juice.

- ▶ PREP TIME: 15 minutes
- ▶ COOK TIME: 1 minute
- ▶ TOTAL TIME: 4 hours, or overnight

MINI LEMON CHEESECAKES IN A JAR

This recipe makes twelve little cheesecakes that are perfect for your next bridal or baby shower—or just to tuck away in the freezer for whenever your sweet tooth strikes.

1 cup (142 g) Lemon Oreo cookie crumbs (about 12 cookies, crushed)

2 packages (8 ounces, or 225 g, each) cream cheese, at room temperature

½ cup (100 g) sugar

¼ cup (60 g) sour cream

1 tablespoon (15 ml) freshly squeezed lemon juice

2 teaspoons grated lemon zest, plus more for garnishing (optional)

½ teaspoon vanilla extract

2 large eggs, at room temperature

Lemon Curd (page 153)

Equally divide the crushed Oreo cookie crumbs among twelve (4-ounce, or 120 ml) canning jars. Use a tamper to evenly flatten the crumbs on the bottom of the jars.

In a large bowl, with a handheld electric mixer, mix the cream cheese and sugar on medium speed until smooth. Blend in the sour cream, lemon juice, lemon zest, and vanilla until combined. One at a time, add the eggs and mix just until combined. Do not overmix. Equally divide the batter among the jars.

Pour 1 cup (235 ml) of water into the pressure cooking pot and place a trivet in the bottom. Carefully place 6 filled jars on the trivet. Place a second trivet on top of the jars and place the remaining 6 jars on top. Lock the lid in place and turn the pressure release valve to the Sealed position. Select High Pressure and 1 minute cook time.

When the cook time ends, turn off the pressure cooker. Let the pressure release naturally. When the valve drops, carefully remove the lid.

Transfer the jars to a wire rack to cool. Soak up any water that may have collected on top of the cheesecakes with the corner of a paper towel. When the cheesecakes are cool, cover with canning jar lids and refrigerate for at least 4 hours, or overnight.

Served topped with a dollop of lemon curd and more grated lemon zest, if desired.

YIELD: 6 to 8 servings

- ▶ TIP: Cheesecake freezes very well, so you can easily make these ahead of time, pop them in the freezer, and let them thaw in the fridge overnight the day before you want to serve them.

CHANGE IT UP!
Add a few drops of food coloring to the cheesecake batter to make these cheesecakes pink or blue for a baby shower. Substitute fresh raspberries or blueberries with whipped cream for the lemon curd or use the Triple Berry Pie Filling (page 155).

Lava Cakes

There is nothing like cutting into a lava cake and seeing that ooey-gooey center trickle onto your plate. The pressure cooker helps these cakes maintain that warm, fudgy center and easily come out of the ramekin (they don't stick as much as oven-cooked cakes).

▶ Chocolate Peanut Butter Lava Cakes with Brûléed Bananas   60

▶ Dark Chocolate Salted Caramel Lava Cakes   62

▶ Dulce de Leche Lava Cakes   65

▶ German Chocolate Lava Cakes   66

▶ S'more Lava Cakes   68

▶ White Chocolate and Nutella Lava Cakes   70

▶ White Chocolate Macadamia Lava Cakes   71

▶ White Chocolate Peppermint Lava Cakes   72

◀ White Chocolate and Nutella Lava Cakes, page 71

CHOCOLATE PEANUT BUTTER LAVA CAKES WITH BRÛLÉED BANANAS

Chocolate, peanut butter, and bananas were made for each other, and together they make an absolutely indulgent lava cake!

Nonstick cooking spray, for preparing the ramekins

6 ounces (170 g) high-quality semisweet chocolate, chopped

½ cup (1 stick, or 112 g) unsalted butter

¼ teaspoon salt

1 teaspoon vanilla extract

3 large eggs

3 large egg yolks

1½ cups (180 g) powdered sugar

½ cup (62 g) all-purpose flour

6 tablespoons (96 g) creamy or crunchy peanut butter, divided

FOR BRÛLÉED BANANAS

2 bananas, sliced

½ cup (100 g) sugar

Vanilla ice cream, for serving

Coat the bottom and sides of six (6-ounce, or 180 ml) ramekins with nonstick cooking spray.

In a small saucepan over medium heat, melt the chocolate and butter together, stirring constantly until smooth. Remove from the heat and stir in the salt and vanilla. Set aside to cool.

In a medium bowl, combine the eggs and egg yolks. Using a handheld electric mixer, beat the eggs on medium-high speed for 1 to 2 minutes until thick and light in color. Whisk in the powdered sugar. Add the cooled chocolate mixture and beat until smooth and incorporated, about 30 seconds. Add the flour and whisk by hand just until combined.

Fill each ramekin two-thirds full of batter. Dollop 1 tablespoon (16 g) of peanut butter into the center of each ramekin and press down just slightly.

Pour 1 cup (235 ml) of water into the pressure cooking pot and place a trivet in the bottom. Carefully place three ramekins on top of the trivet. Lock the lid in place and turn the pressure release valve to the Sealed position. Select High Pressure and 4 minutes cook time.

When the cook time ends, turn off the pressure cooker. Use a quick pressure release. When the valve drops, carefully remove the lid. Check the cakes for doneness: The sides should be set and the centers slightly soft. (If the cake is overcooked, it will still be fudgy and delicious, but it won't have the molten filling.) If the batter still appears runny, relock the lid and cook at High Pressure for 1 minute more, followed by another quick pressure release. Transfer the ramekins to a wire rack to cool.

Add another 1 cup (235 ml) of water to the pressure cooking pot and place the remaining three ramekins on top of the trivet. Repeat the cooking process.

Let the cakes cool for at least 5 minutes. Run a knife around the edge of the cakes. Invert a plate on top of the ramekin and gently flip both the plate and ramekin over, allowing the cake to fall onto the plate. Serve hot with a scoop of vanilla ice cream and the brûléed bananas.

To make the brûléed bananas: Dip one side of each banana slice in the sugar. If using a culinary torch, set the bananas on a plate, sugared-side up. Use the torch to heat the sugar until it bubbles and caramelizes. If not using a torch, place the bananas on a sheet pan, sugared-side up. Move your oven rack to the top position and broil the bananas for 1 to 2 minutes until golden brown. Watch closely because they can go from underdone to burned very quickly.

YIELD: 6 servings

► **TIP:** Though the direct translation of brûlée is "burned," you don't want to burn the bananas black! Although the broiler is practical, it often results in uneven caramelization. You'll have more control over the browning process if you use a flame. You can invest in a kitchen torch, or even a welding torch from the hardware store will work!

DARK CHOCOLATE SALTED CARAMEL LAVA CAKES

Add salted caramel to dark chocolate for a delightfully indulgent dessert. Cut into the cake and just watch as the salted caramel filling flows onto the plate!

Nonstick cooking spray, for preparing the ramekins

6 ounces (170 g) high-quality bittersweet chocolate, chopped

½ cup (1 stick, or 112 g) unsalted butter

1 teaspoon vanilla extract

¼ teaspoon salt

3 large eggs

3 large egg yolks

1½ cups (180 g) powdered sugar

½ cup (62 g) all-purpose flour

6 caramel candies

Dulce de Leche (page 146) or warmed caramel sauce, for serving

Vanilla Whipped Cream (page 148), for serving

Flaky sea salt, for serving

Coat the bottom and sides of six (6-ounce, or 180 ml) ramekins with nonstick cooking spray.

In a small saucepan over medium heat, melt the chocolate and butter together, stirring constantly until smooth. Remove from the heat and stir in the vanilla and salt. Set aside to cool.

In a medium bowl, combine the eggs and egg yolks. With a hand-held electric mixer, beat the eggs on medium-high speed for 1 to 2 minutes until thick and light in color. Whisk in the powdered sugar. Add the cooled chocolate mixture and beat until smooth and incorporated, about 30 seconds. Add the flour and whisk by hand just until combined. Fill each ramekin two-thirds full of batter. Place a caramel candy into the center of each ramekin and press down very slightly.

Pour 1 cup (235 ml) of water into the pressure cooking pot and place a trivet in the bottom. Carefully place three ramekins on top of the trivet. Lock the lid in place and turn the pressure release valve to the Sealed position. Select High Pressure and 4 minutes cook time.

When the cook time ends, turn off the pressure cooker. Use a quick pressure release. When the valve drops, carefully remove the lid. Check the cakes for doneness: The sides should be set and the center slightly soft. (If the cake is overcooked, it will still be moist and delicious, but it won't have the molten filling.) If the batter still appears runny, relock the lid and cook at High Pressure for 1 minute more, followed by another quick pressure release. Transfer the ramekins to a wire rack to cool.

Add another 1 cup (235 ml) of water to the pressure cooking pot and place the remaining three ramekins on the trivet. Repeat the cooking process.

Let the cakes cool for at least 5 minutes. Run a knife around the edge of the cakes. Invert a plate on top of the ramekin and gently flip both the plate and ramekin over, allowing the cake to fall onto the plate. Serve hot with a drizzle of Dulce de Leche, Vanilla Whipped Cream, and a sprinkle of sea salt.

YIELD: 6 servings

> **TIP:** Not a dark chocolate fan? Swap the bittersweet chocolate for milk or semisweet chocolate for a sweeter cake.

DULCE DE LECHE LAVA CAKES

Dulce de Leche flavors this cake with sweet, luscious caramel from the inside out. Add a pinch of flaky sea salt to the top of the finished cake for the perfect sweet and salty bite.

Nonstick cooking spray, for preparing the ramekins

6 ounces (180 g) Dulce de Leche (page 146)

½ cup (1 stick, or 112 g) unsalted butter

1 teaspoon vanilla extract

¼ teaspoon salt

3 large eggs

3 large egg yolks

1½ cups (180 g) powdered sugar

½ cup (62 g) all-purpose flour

Pralines and caramel ice cream, for serving

Coat the bottom and sides of six (6-ounce, or 180 ml) ramekins with nonstick cooking spray.

In a small saucepan over medium heat, melt the Dulce de Leche and butter together, stirring constantly until smooth. Remove from the heat and stir in the vanilla and salt. Set aside to cool.

In a medium bowl, combine the eggs and egg yolks. With a hand-held electric mixer, beat the eggs on medium-high speed for 1 to 2 minutes until thick and light in color. Whisk in the powdered sugar. Add the cooled Dulce de Leche mixture and beat until smooth and incorporated, about 30 seconds. Add the flour and whisk by hand just until combined. Fill each ramekin two-thirds full of batter.

Pour 1 cup (235 ml) of water into the pressure cooking pot and place a trivet in the bottom. Carefully place three ramekins on top of the trivet. Lock the lid in place and turn the pressure release valve to the Sealed position. Select High Pressure and 4 minutes cook time.

When the cook time ends, turn off the pressure cooker. Use a quick pressure release. When the valve drops, carefully remove the lid. Check the cakes for doneness: The sides should be set and the center slightly soft. (If the cake is overcooked, it will still be moist and delicious, but it won't have the molten filling.) If the batter still appears runny, relock the lid and cook at High Pressure for 1 minute more, followed by another quick pressure release. Transfer the ramekins to a wire rack to cool.

Add another 1 cup (235 ml) of water to the pressure cooking pot and place the remaining three ramekins on top of the trivet. Repeat the cooking process.

Let the cakes cool for at least 5 minutes. Run a knife around the edge of the cakes. Invert a plate on top of the ramekin and gently flip both the plate and ramekin over, allowing the cake to fall onto the plate. Serve hot with a scoop of pralines and caramel ice cream.

YIELD: 6 servings

- **TIP:** Either canned or homemade dulce de leche will work here. For a fun twist, make this with the Salted Chocolate Dulce de Leche (page 147).

GERMAN CHOCOLATE LAVA CAKES

Taking a spin from the classic German chocolate cake, this lava cake is filled with sweet coconut pecan frosting and garnished with toasted coconut and pecans to satisfy that sweet tooth.

Nonstick cooking spray, for preparing the ramekins

6 ounces (170 g) high-quality bittersweet chocolate, chopped

½ cup (1 stick, or 112 g) unsalted butter

¼ teaspoon salt

1 teaspoon vanilla extract

3 large eggs

3 large egg yolks

1½ cups (180 g) powdered sugar

½ cup (62 g) all-purpose flour

6 tablespoons (90 g) Coconut-Pecan Frosting (page 144), plus more for serving

Chocolate ice cream, toasted coconut, and pecans, for serving

Coat the bottom and sides of six (6-ounce, or 180 ml) ramekins with nonstick cooking spray.

In a small saucepan over medium heat, melt the chocolate and butter together, stirring constantly until smooth. Remove from heat and stir in the salt and vanilla. Set aside to cool.

In a medium bowl, combine the eggs and egg yolks. Using a handheld electric mixer, beat the eggs on medium-high speed for 1 to 2 minutes until thick and light in color. Whisk in the powdered sugar. Add the cooled chocolate mixture and beat until smooth and incorporated, about 30 seconds. Add the flour and whisk by hand just until combined.

Fill each ramekin two-thirds full of batter. Dollop 1 tablespoon (15 g) of frosting into the center of each ramekin and press down just slightly.

Pour 1 cup (235 ml) of water into the pressure cooking pot and place a trivet in the bottom. Carefully place three ramekins on top of the trivet. Lock the lid in place and turn the pressure release valve to the Sealed position. Select High Pressure and 4 minutes cook time.

When the cook time ends, turn off the pressure cooker. Use a quick pressure release. When the valve drops, carefully remove the lid. Check the cakes for doneness: The sides should be set and the center slightly soft. (If the cake is overcooked, it will still be fudgy and delicious, but it won't have the molten filling.) If the batter still appears runny, relock the lid and cook at High Pressure for 1 minute more, followed by another quick pressure release. Transfer the ramekins to a wire rack to cool.

Add another 1 cup (235 ml) of water to the pressure cooker cooking pot and place the remaining three ramekins on top of the trivet. Repeat the cooking process.

Let the cakes cool for at least 5 minutes. Run a knife around the edges of the cakes. Invert a plate on top of the ramekin and gently flip both the plate and ramekin over, allowing the cake to fall onto the plate.

Serve hot with a scoop of chocolate ice cream, an extra drizzle of frosting, and a sprinkle of pecans and toasted coconut.

YIELD: 6 servings

▶ **TIP:** Toasted coconut is available in stores in both sweetened and unsweetened varieties, but you can easily make your own at home. Simply add coconut to a sauté pan and cook over medium heat, lightly stirring until the coconut starts to brown. It can burn quickly so watch it closely.

S'MORE LAVA CAKES

Classic s'more flavors get an amazing makeover here! This lava cake is filled with marshmallow cream and garnished with a crumble of graham cracker crumbs.

Nonstick cooking spray, for preparing the ramekins

6 ounces (170 g) high-quality semisweet chocolate, chopped

½ cup (1 stick, or 112 g) unsalted butter

1 teaspoon vanilla extract

⅛ teaspoon kosher salt

3 large eggs

3 large egg yolks

1½ cups (180 g) powdered sugar

½ cup (62 g) all-purpose flour

6 tablespoons (36 g) marshmallow cream, divided

Vanilla Whipped Cream (page 148) or ice cream, for serving

Graham cracker crumbs, for serving

Coat the bottom and sides of six (6-ounce, or 180 ml) ramekins with nonstick cooking spray.

In a small saucepan over medium heat, melt the chocolate and butter together, stirring constantly until smooth. Remove from the heat and stir in the vanilla and salt. Set aside to cool.

In a medium bowl, combine the eggs and egg yolks. With a hand-held electric mixer, beat the eggs on medium-high speed for 1 to 2 minutes until thick and light in color. Whisk in the powdered sugar. Add the cooled chocolate mixture and beat until smooth and incorporated, about 30 seconds. Add the flour and whisk by hand just until combined. Fill each ramekin two-thirds full of batter. Dollop 1 tablespoon (6 g) of marshmallow cream into the center of each ramekin and press down very slightly.

Pour 1 cup (235 ml) of water into the pressure cooking pot and place a trivet in the bottom. Carefully place three ramekins on top of the trivet. Lock the lid in place and turn the pressure release valve to the Sealed position. Select High Pressure and 4 minutes cook time.

When the cook time ends, turn off the pressure cooker. Use a quick pressure release. When the valve drops, carefully remove the lid. Check the cakes for doneness: The sides should be set and the center slightly soft. (If the cake is overcooked, it will still be moist and delicious, but it won't have the molten filling.) If the batter still appears runny, relock the lid and cook at High Pressure for 1 minute more, followed by another quick pressure release. Transfer the ramekins to a wire rack to cool.

Add another 1 cup (235 ml) of water to the pressure cooker cooking pot and place the remaining three ramekins on top of the trivet. Repeat the cooking process.

Let the cakes cool for at least 5 minutes. Run a knife around the edge of the cakes. Invert a plate on top of the ramekin and gently flip both the plate and ramekin over, allowing the cake to fall onto the plate. Serve hot with a scoop of Vanilla Whipped Cream or vanilla ice cream and a sprinkle of graham cracker crumbs.

YIELD: 6 servings

▶ **TIP:** Warm some jarred marshmallow cream and drizzle it over the lava cakes for even *s'more* goodness!

WHITE CHOCOLATE AND NUTELLA LAVA CAKES

What could make Nutella even better? Eating it warm in a sweet white chocolate lava cake! The extra hazelnut crunch is the perfect touch.

Nonstick cooking spray, for preparing the ramekins

6 ounces (170 g) high-quality white chocolate, chopped

½ cup (1 stick, or 112 g) unsalted butter

¼ teaspoon salt

1 teaspoon vanilla extract

3 large eggs

3 large egg yolks

1 cup (120 g) powdered sugar

¾ cup (94 g) all-purpose flour

3 tablespoons (21 g) chopped hazelnuts, plus more for serving

6 tablespoons (111 g) Nutella, divided

Chocolate ice cream, for serving

Coat the bottom and sides of six (6-ounce, or 180 ml) ramekins with nonstick cooking spray.

In a small saucepan over medium heat, melt the white chocolate and butter together, stirring constantly until smooth. Remove from the heat and stir in the salt and vanilla. Set aside to cool.

In a medium bowl, combine the eggs and egg yolks. Using a handheld electric mixer, beat the eggs on medium-high speed for 1 to 2 minutes until thick and light in color. Whisk in the powdered sugar. Add the cooled chocolate mixture and beat until smooth and incorporated, about 30 seconds. Add the flour and whisk by hand just until combined.

Fill each ramekin two-thirds full of batter. Put 1 tablespoon (18 g) of Nutella on the center of each and press down slightly.

Pour 1 cup (235 ml) of water into the pressure cooking pot and place a trivet in the bottom. Place three ramekins on top of the trivet. Lock the lid in place and turn the pressure release valve to the Sealed position. Select High Pressure and 4 minutes cook time.

When the cook time ends, turn off the pressure cooker. Use a quick pressure release. When the valve drops, carefully remove the lid. Check the cakes for doneness: The sides should be set and the center slightly soft. (If the cake is overcooked, it will still be moist and delicious, but it won't have the molten filling.) If the batter still appears runny, relock the lid and cook at High Pressure for 1 minute more, followed by another quick pressure release. Transfer the ramekins to a wire rack to cool.

Add another 1 cup (235 ml) of water to the pressure cooking pot and place the remaining three ramekins on top of the trivet. Repeat the cooking process.

Let the cakes cool for at least 5 minutes. Run a knife around the edges of the cakes. Invert a plate on top of the ramekin and gently flip both the plate and ramekin over, allowing the cake to fall onto the plate. Serve hot with a scoop of chocolate ice cream and an extra sprinkle of hazelnuts.

YIELD: 6 servings

► **TIP:** Use a small cookie scoop to portion Nutella evenly into the center of each cake.

- ▶ PREP TIME: 15 minutes
- ▶ COOK TIME: 8 minutes
- ▶ TOTAL TIME: 25 minutes

WHITE CHOCOLATE MACADAMIA LAVA CAKES

White chocolate and macadamia nuts aren't just for cookies. This sweet-and-salty lava cake will prove it!

Nonstick cooking spray, for preparing the ramekins

6 ounces (170 g) high-quality white chocolate, chopped

½ cup (1 stick, or 112 g) unsalted butter

¼ teaspoon salt

1 teaspoon vanilla extract

3 large eggs

3 large egg yolks

1 cup (120 g) powdered sugar

¾ cup (94 g) all-purpose flour

6 white chocolate truffle balls (see Tip)

3 tablespoons (25 g) chopped roasted salted macadamia nuts, plus more for serving

Vanilla bean ice cream, for serving

Coat the bottom and sides of six (6-ounce, or 180 ml) ramekins with nonstick cooking spray.

In a small saucepan over medium heat, melt the white chocolate and butter together, stirring constantly until smooth. Remove from heat and stir in the salt and vanilla. Set aside to cool.

In a medium bowl, combine the eggs and egg yolks. Using a handheld electric mixer, beat the eggs on medium-high speed for 1 to 2 minutes until thick and light in color. Whisk in the powdered sugar. Add the cooled chocolate mixture and beat until smooth and incorporated, about 30 seconds. Add the flour and whisk by hand just until combined.

Fill each ramekin two-thirds full of batter. Place a white chocolate truffle ball into the center of each ramekin and press down just slightly. Sprinkle each ramekin with chopped macadamia nuts.

Pour 1 cup (235 ml) of water into the pressure cooking pot and place a trivet in the bottom. Carefully place three ramekins on top of the trivet. Lock the lid in place and turn the pressure release valve to the Sealed position. Select High Pressure and 4 minutes cook time.

When the cook time ends, turn off the pressure cooker. Use a quick pressure release. When the valve drops, carefully remove the lid. Check the cakes for doneness: The sides should be set and the center slightly soft. (If the cake is overcooked, it will still be moist and delicious, but it won't have the molten filling.) If the batter still appears runny, relock the lid and cook at High Pressure for 1 minute more, followed by another quick pressure release. Transfer the ramekins to a wire rack to cool.

Add another 1 cup (235 ml) of water to the pressure cooking pot and place the remaining three ramekins on top of the trivet. Repeat the cooking process.

Let the cakes cool for at least 5 minutes. Run a knife around the edges of the cakes. Invert a plate on top of the ramekin and gently flip both the plate and ramekin over, allowing the cake to fall onto the plate. Serve hot with a scoop of vanilla bean ice cream and an extra sprinkle of macadamia nuts.

YIELD: 6 servings

▶ **TIP:** The white chocolate truffles create an extra-rich white chocolate lava, but they can be omitted if desired.

▸ PREP TIME: 15 minutes

▸ COOK TIME: 8 minutes

▸ TOTAL TIME: 28 minutes

WHITE CHOCOLATE PEPPERMINT LAVA CAKES

This lava cake has the perfect blend of sweet white chocolate and cool peppermint. The peppermint lava and crunchy candy really add to the fun factor here!

Nonstick cooking spray, for preparing the ramekins

6 ounces (170 g) high-quality white chocolate, chopped

½ cup (1 stick, or 112 g) unsalted butter

1 teaspoon vanilla extract

1 teaspoon peppermint extract

¼ teaspoon salt

3 large eggs

3 large egg yolks

1 cup (120 g) powdered sugar

¾ cup (94 g) all-purpose flour

3 tablespoons (32 g) crushed peppermint candy, plus more for serving

6 peppermint or white chocolate truffle balls

Peppermint or vanilla ice cream, for serving

Coat the bottom and sides of six (6-ounce, or 180 ml) ramekins with nonstick cooking spray.

In a small saucepan over medium heat, melt the white chocolate and butter together, stirring constantly until smooth. Remove from the heat and stir in vanilla extract, peppermint extract, and salt. Set aside to cool.

In a medium bowl, combine the eggs and egg yolks. With a hand-held electric mixer, beat the eggs on medium-high speed for 1 to 2 minutes until thick and light in color. Whisk in the powdered sugar. Add the cooled chocolate mixture and beat until smooth and incorporated, about 30 seconds. Add the flour and whisk by hand just until combined. Fill each ramekin two-thirds full of batter.

Place a peppermint or white chocolate truffle ball into the center of each ramekin and press it down slightly. Sprinkle each ramekin with crushed peppermint candy.

Pour 1 cup (235 ml) of water into the pressure cooking pot and place a trivet in the bottom. Carefully place three ramekins on top of the trivet. Lock the lid in place and turn the pressure release valve to the Sealed position. Select High Pressure and 4 minutes cook time.

When the cook time ends, turn off the pressure cooker. Use a quick pressure release. When the valve drops, carefully remove the lid. Check the cakes for doneness: The sides should be set and the center slightly soft. (If the cake is overcooked, it will still be moist and delicious, but it won't have the molten filling.) If the batter still appears runny, relock the lid and cook at High Pressure for 1 minute more, followed by another quick pressure release. Transfer the ramekins to a wire rack to cool.

Add another 1 cup (235 ml) of water to the pressure cooker cooking pot and place the remaining three ramekins on top of the trivet. Repeat the cooking process.

Let the cakes cool for at least 5 minutes. Run a knife around the edge of the cakes. Invert a plate on top of the ramekin and gently flip both the plate and ramekin over, allowing the cake to fall onto the plate. Serve hot with a scoop of peppermint or vanilla ice cream and an extra sprinkle of crushed peppermint candy.

YIELD: 6 servings

▶ **TIP:** Store-bought crushed peppermint candy is uniform in size and makes this cake more convenient to make.

Cakes

Whether for a birthday party or an ordinary weeknight, cakes are a perfect ending to the day! With the pressure cooker, you get moist, tender cakes in a fraction of the time—without turning on the oven.

▶ Lemon Poppy Seed Cake   76

▶ Angel Food Cake   77

▶ Raisin-Pecan Spice Cake   79
  with Dulce de Leche Drizzle

▶ Chocolate-Raspberry Cake for Two   80

▶ Caramel Walnut Brownie Pudding Cake   81

▶ Chocolate Lover's Dream Cake   82

▶ Cinnamon Tres Leches Cake   84
  with Macerated Strawberries

▶ German Chocolate Cake   86

◀ German Chocolate Cake, page 86

LEMON POPPY SEED CAKE

This sunny cake has a bright lemon flavor and is so moist and delicious no one will ever guess it started with a mix.

FOR CAKE

Nonstick cooking spray, for preparing the pan

8 ounces (225 g) boxed lemon cake with pudding in the mix

2 large eggs

½ cup (120 ml) water

¼ cup (60 ml) vegetable oil

¼ cup (60 g) sour cream

2 teaspoons poppy seeds

FOR LEMON GLAZE

½ cup (60 g) powdered sugar

2 teaspoons freshly squeezed lemon juice

To make the cake: Coat a half-size Bundt pan with nonstick cooking spray.

In a large bowl, combine the cake mix, eggs, water, vegetable oil, and sour cream. Stir to combine for 2 minutes. Stir in the poppy seeds. Spoon the batter into the prepared pan. Cover the pan with a paper towel and cover the paper towel completely with aluminum foil, crimped around the edges to seal.

Pour 1 cup (235 ml) of water into the pressure cooking pot and place a trivet in the bottom. Carefully center the filled pan on a sling and lower the pan onto the trivet. Lock the lid in place and turn the pressure release valve to the Sealed position. Select High Pressure and 20 minutes cook time.

When the cook time ends, turn off the pressure cooker. Let the pressure release naturally for 10 minutes, and finish with a quick pressure release. When the valve drops, carefully remove the lid.

With the sling, transfer the pan to a wire rack. Remove the foil and paper towel. Cool the cake, uncovered, for 5 minutes. Gently loosen the edges, remove the cake from the pan, and cool completely on a wire rack.

To make the lemon glaze: In a small bowl, stir together the powdered sugar and lemon juice until smooth. Drizzle the glaze over the cooled cake just before serving.

YIELD: 6 to 8 servings

> **TIP:** Freeze leftover lemon juice in an ice cube tray to use another day. One ice cube is approximately 1 tablespoon (15 ml) of juice.

▸ PREP TIME: 15 minutes

▸ COOK TIME: 27 minutes

▸ TOTAL TIME: 2 hours,
  30 minutes

ANGEL FOOD CAKE

Light, moist, and soft, this pressure cooker version of angel food cake is absolutely "heavenly!" Serve it with glazed strawberries, chocolate syrup, or eat it plain—it's a treat any way you serve it.

¾ cup (96 g) cake flour

1 cup plus 2 tablespoons (226 g) sugar, divided

9 large egg whites

¼ teaspoon salt

1¼ teaspoons cream of tartar

1 teaspoon vanilla extract

½ teaspoon almond extract (optional)

Vanilla Whipped Cream (page 148), for serving

Fresh sliced strawberries, for serving

In a medium bowl, whisk the cake flour and ½ cup plus 2 tablespoons (126 g) of sugar. Set aside.

In a large bowl, combine the egg whites, salt, cream of tartar, vanilla, and almond extract (if using). With a handheld electric mixer, beat the egg whites on medium speed until barely frothy. Sprinkle ¼ cup (50 g) of sugar over the egg whites. Beat again on medium speed until incorporated. Add the remaining ¼ cup (50 g) of sugar and continue to beat until the mixture forms stiff, glossy peaks.

Gently fold half the dry ingredients into the beaten egg whites. Once combined, add the remaining dry ingredients and gently fold them into the batter until combined. Spoon the batter into an ungreased 7-inch (18 cm) tube pan. It will be full. Cover with aluminum foil and lightly crimp it around the edges of the pan.

Pour 1 cup (235 ml) of water into the pressure cooking pot and place a trivet in the bottom. Carefully center the filled pan on a sling and lower the pan onto the trivet. Fold the sling down so the lid will close. Lock the lid in place and turn the pressure release valve to the Sealed position. Select High Pressure and 27 minutes cook time.

When the cook time ends, turn off the pressure cooker. Let the pressure release naturally for 10 minutes, and finish with a quick pressure release. When the valve drops, carefully remove the lid.

With the sling, carefully remove the tube pan and set it upside-down on a heat-resistant surface to cool for 90 minutes. (This step is important—don't rush it!)

Once cool, run a knife around the sides and the center of the pan to remove the cake. Serve immediately with Vanilla Whipped Cream and strawberries, or any of the sauces and compotes from pages 132 to 155. Store leftovers at room temperature in a sealed container for up to 1 week.

YIELD: 8 servings

▸ **TIP:** Angel food cakes are traditionally cooked in a tube pan. If you don't have one, this recipe will also work in a half-size Bundt pan; the cake won't be as tall.

RAISIN-PECAN SPICE CAKE WITH DULCE DE LECHE DRIZZLE

An old-fashioned spice cake loaded with raisins and pecans, this half-size Bundt cake is a perfect finish to dinner any night of the week.

Nonstick cooking spray, for preparing the pan

1¾ cups (189 g) boxed yellow cake mix

2 large eggs

½ cup (120 ml) water

¼ cup (60 ml) vegetable oil

¼ cup (60 g) sour cream

1 teaspoon ground cinnamon

½ teaspoon ground allspice

⅛ teaspoon ground nutmeg

½ cup (56 g) toasted pecans, chopped, plus more for garnishing (optional)

½ cup (75 g) raisins

2 tablespoons (16 g) all-purpose flour

Dulce de Leche (page 146; optional)

Coat a half-size Bundt pan with nonstick cooking spray.

In a large bowl, combine the cake mix, eggs, water, vegetable oil, sour cream, cinnamon, allspice, and nutmeg. Stir to combine for 2 minutes. In a small zip-top bag, toss together the pecans, raisins, and flour. Add to the cake batter and stir to combine. Spoon the batter into the prepared pan. Cover the pan with a paper towel and cover the paper towel completely with aluminum foil, crimped around the edges to seal.

Pour 1 cup (235 ml) of water into the pressure cooking pot and place a trivet in the bottom. Center the Bundt pan on a sling and lower it onto the trivet. Lock the lid in place and turn the pressure release valve to the Sealed position. Select High Pressure and 20 minutes cook time.

When the cook time ends, turn off the pressure cooker. Let the pressure release naturally for 10 minutes, and finish with a quick pressure release. When the valve drops, carefully remove the lid.

With the sling, transfer the pan to a wire rack. Remove the foil and paper towel. Cool for 5 minutes, uncovered. Gently loosen the edges, remove the cake from the pan, and cool completely on a wire rack.

If desired, decorate the cake with a drizzle of warmed Dulce de Leche and chopped pecans.

YIELD: 6 to 8 servings

> **TIP:** If you're not a fan of raisins, use your favorite dried fruit or double the pecans.

▸ PREP TIME: 5 minutes

▸ COOK TIME: 9 minutes

▸ TOTAL TIME: 45 minutes

CHOCOLATE-RASPBERRY CAKE FOR TWO

This is a perfect cake for Valentine's Day, anniversaries, or any night you're having a special celebration just for two.

Nonstick cooking spray, for preparing the pans

1 cup (108 g) boxed devil's food cake mix

1 large egg yolk

¼ cup (60 ml) water

2 tablespoons (30 ml) vegetable oil

1 tablespoon (15 g) sour cream

½ recipe Chocolate Ganache (page 139)

1 pint (250 g) fresh raspberries

Powdered sugar, for decorating

Coat two 4-inch (10 cm) cake pans with nonstick cooking spray.

In a large bowl, whisk together the cake mix, egg yolk, water, vegetable oil, and sour cream until blended, about 30 seconds. Divide the batter between the prepared pans. Cover the pans with aluminum foil coated with nonstick cooking spray.

Pour 1 cup (235 ml) of water into the pressure cooking pot and place a trivet in the bottom. Carefully center one cake pan on the trivet. Put a second trivet on top of the cake pan and place the second cake pan on top of the second trivet. Lock the lid in place and turn the pressure release valve to the Sealed position. Select High Pressure and 9 minutes cook time.

When the cook time ends, turn off the pressure cooker. Let the pressure release naturally for 10 minutes, and finish with a quick pressure release. When the valve drops, carefully remove the lid. Transfer the pans to a wire rack to cool for 5 minutes. Invert the cakes onto the rack to cool completely.

If the cakes are domed, use a sharp knife to cut off the tops of the cakes so they are flat. Carefully spoon Chocolate Ganache on top of each cake and let it drizzle down the sides. Pile half the raspberries on each cake and finish with a sprinkle of powdered sugar.

YIELD: 2 servings

> **TIP:** This cake is the perfect size for a smash cake or to give as a special birthday treat.

CARAMEL WALNUT BROWNIE PUDDING CAKE

This ooey-gooey brownie pudding cake is sprinkled with caramels and walnuts. Its deep, rich chocolate flavor is at its best paired with a scoop of vanilla ice cream.

Nonstick cooking spray, for preparing the pan

1 package (18 ounces, or 510 g) boxed brownie mix

1 teaspoon baking powder

2 large eggs

5 tablespoons (70 g) unsalted butter, melted

¼ cup (60 ml) milk

¼ cup (60 g) packed brown sugar

¼ cup (22 g) cocoa powder

8 caramel candies

¼ cup (30 g) chopped walnuts

¼ cup (60 ml) boiling water

Vanilla ice cream, for serving

Coat a 7-inch (18 cm) cake pan with nonstick cooking spray.

In a small bowl, combine the brownie mix and baking powder.

In a large bowl, whisk together the eggs, butter, and milk until blended. Add the dry ingredients and whisk until combined. Scrape the batter into the prepared pan. Sprinkle with the brown sugar and then the cocoa powder. Top with the caramels and walnuts (don't stir). Pour the boiling water over the cocoa powder.

Pour 1 cup (235 ml) of water into the pressure cooking pot and place a trivet in the bottom. Carefully center the filled pan on a sling and lower the pan onto the trivet. Fold the sling down so the lid will close. Lock the lid in place and turn the pressure release valve to the Sealed position. Select High Pressure and 40 minutes cook time.

When the cook time ends, turn off the pressure cooker. Let the pressure release naturally for 10 minutes, and finish with a quick pressure release. When the valve drops, carefully remove the lid. The top of the brownies should be set with a thick pudding layer underneath. If the top layer is still wet, relock the lid and cook at High Pressure for 5 to 10 minutes more.

With the sling, carefully transfer the cake pan to a wire rack and let cool, uncovered, for 10 minutes. Spoon the warm brownie pudding into bowls and top with a scoop of vanilla ice cream.

YIELD: 8 servings

> **TIP:** If you prefer to use a high-quality specialty caramel in place of the individually wrapped caramel candies, use a 2-ounce (55 g) block of caramel cut into 8 pieces.

CHOCOLATE LOVER'S DREAM CAKE

Layer upon layer of chocolate makes this cake every chocolate lover's dream come true. This will be the star of any party!

FOR CAKE

Nonstick cooking spray, for preparing the pan

1 box (15.25 ounces) milk or dark chocolate cake mix (plus the ingredients it calls for)

FOR CHOCOLATE SAUCE

1 can (14 ounces, or 425 ml) sweetened condensed milk

¾ cup (217 g) chocolate fudge topping

FOR CHOCOLATE WHIPPED CREAM

2 cups (475 ml) heavy cream

¼ cup (22 g) cocoa powder

½ cup (60 g) powdered sugar

½ teaspoon vanilla extract

FOR TOPPING

½ cup (75 g) toffee bits

To make the cake: Coat a 7-inch (18 cm) cake pan with nonstick cooking spray.

In a large bowl, prepare the chocolate cake mix according to the package directions. Pour the batter into the prepared cake pan and smooth the top.

Pour 1 cup (235 ml) of water into the pressure cooking pot and place a trivet in the bottom. Carefully center the filled pan on a sling and lower the pan onto the trivet. Fold the sling down so the lid will close. Lock the lid in place and turn the pressure release valve to the Sealed position. Select High Pressure and 35 minutes cook time.

When the cook time ends, turn off the pressure cooker. Let the pressure release naturally. When the valve drops, carefully remove the lid.

With the sling, carefully transfer the pan to a wire rack to cool.

To make the chocolate sauce: In a medium bowl, whisk the sweetened condensed milk and chocolate fudge topping to combine. If needed, warm the ingredients for 30 seconds in the microwave at high power. Reserve about one-fourth of the sauce for serving. Using a fork, skewer, or the handle of a thin wooden spoon, poke several holes in the top of the cake. Pour the remaining three-fourths of the chocolate sauce over the cake, letting it soak in with each drizzle. Cover and refrigerate for at least 2 hours until chilled.

To make the chocolate whipped cream: In a medium bowl, with a handheld electric mixer, beat the cream on medium speed until it starts to thicken. Add the cocoa powder, powdered sugar, and vanilla. Beat again until thick. Spread the chocolate whipped cream over the cake and sprinkle the toffee bits over the cream. Serve cold with a drizzle of the reserved chocolate sauce.

YIELD: 8 servings

> **TIP:** This cake is best eaten the same day it's prepared. If you need to make it the day before, "bake" the cake in the pressure cooker and poke the holes in it. Prepare the chocolate sauce and refrigerate. The next day, warm the chocolate sauce in the microwave and it pour on top of the cake. Continue with the recipe as directed.

CINNAMON TRES LECHES CAKE WITH MACERATED STRAWBERRIES

This cinnamon-flavored tres leches cake is like a refreshing drink of sweet milk with every bite. The macerated strawberries are a perfect sweet-tart pairing to the cool, rich cake.

FOR CAKE

Nonstick cooking spray, for preparing the pan

5 large eggs, separated

1 cup (200 g) sugar, divided

⅓ cup (80 ml) milk

1 tablespoon vanilla extract

1 cup (125 g) all-purpose flour

1 tablespoon (14 g) baking powder

¼ teaspoon salt

½ teaspoon ground Vietnamese cinnamon

FOR TRES LECHES SAUCE

1 can (14 ounces, or 425 ml) sweetened condensed milk

1 can (12 ounces, or 355 ml) evaporated milk

½ cup (120 ml) half-and-half

1 teaspoon ground Vietnamese cinnamon

FOR MACERATED STRAWBERRIES

1 pint (340 g) sliced strawberries

1 tablespoon (13 g) sugar

½ teaspoon vanilla extract

Vanilla Whipped Cream (page 148), for serving

To make the cake: Coat a 7-inch (18 cm) cake pan with nonstick cooking spray.

In a large bowl, combine the egg yolks and ¾ cup (150 g) of sugar. Using a handheld electric mixer, beat the ingredients on medium-high speed until pale yellow and doubled in volume, about 3 or 4 minutes. Scrape the sides of the bowl. Add the milk, vanilla, flour, baking powder, salt, and cinnamon. Beat on low speed just until combined.

In a second bowl, beat the egg whites using an electric handheld mixer on medium-high speed until soft peaks form. Sprinkle in the remaining ¼ cup (50 g) of sugar and beat until stiff peaks form.

Gently fold the egg white mixture into the cake batter until combined. Spoon the batter into the prepared cake pan and smooth the top.

Pour 1 cup (235 ml) of water into the pressure cooking pot and place a trivet in the bottom. Carefully center the filled pan on a sling and lower the pan into the cooking pot. Fold the sling down so the lid will close. Lock the lid in place and turn the pressure release valve to the Sealed position. Select High Pressure and 45 minutes cook time.

When the cook time ends, turn off the pressure cooker. Let the pressure release naturally for 15 minutes, and finish with a quick pressure release. When the valve drops, carefully remove the lid. With the sling, transfer the pan to a wire rack to cool.

To make the Tres Leches Sauce:
In a medium bowl, whisk the sweetened condensed milk, evaporated milk, half-and-half, and cinnamon until well combined. Reserve about one-fourth of the mixture for serving.

Using a fork, skewer, or the handle of a thin wooden spoon, poke several holes all over the top of the cake. Slowly pour the remaining three-fourths of the Tres Leches Sauce over the cake, allowing it to soak in with each drizzle. Cover the cake and refrigerate until chilled and the milk has soaked in, at least 3 hours.

To make the Macerated Strawberries: About 30 to 60 minutes before serving, in a large bowl, stir together the strawberries, sugar, and vanilla. Cover and refrigerate until the strawberries have released some of their liquid.

Serve the cake cold with a dollop of Vanilla Whipped Cream, a spoonful of Macerated Strawberries, and a splash of the reserved Tres Leches Sauce.

YIELD: 8 servings

▸ **TIP:** "Macerated" is just a fancy way to indicate fruit has been soaked in liquid to make it softer and sweeter. In the case of these strawberries, the liquid is released by the strawberries themselves once the sugar is added. If you wish, use frozen strawberries in this recipe—just thaw and sweeten to taste.

GERMAN CHOCOLATE CAKE

This light and fluffy shortcut cake starts with half of a boxed cake mix. And, the cute little 7-inch (18 cm) size makes it perfect for an anytime sweet snack.

Nonstick cooking spray, for preparing the pan

8 ounces (225 g) boxed German chocolate cake mix with pudding in the mix

1 large egg

1 large egg yolk

½ cup (120 ml) water

¼ cup (60 ml) vegetable oil

¼ (60 g) cup sour cream

1 teaspoon vanilla extract

Coconut-Pecan Frosting (page 144)

Coat a 7 × 3-inch (18 × 7.5 cm) cake pan with nonstick cooking spray.

In a large bowl, whisk together the cake mix, egg, egg yolk, water, vegetable oil, and sour cream for 2 minutes to combine. Spoon the batter into the prepared pan. Cover the pan with a paper towel and cover the paper towel completely with aluminum foil, crimping it around the edges to seal.

Pour 1 cup (235 ml) of water into the pressure cooking pot and place a trivet in the bottom. Carefully center the filled pan on a sling and lower the pan onto the trivet. Fold the sling down so the lid will close. Lock the lid in place and turn the pressure release valve to the Sealed position. Select High Pressure and 25 minutes cook time.

When the cook time ends, turn off the pressure cooker. Let the pressure release naturally for 10 minutes, and finish with a quick pressure release. When the valve drops, carefully remove the lid.

With the sling, transfer the pan to a wire rack. Remove the foil and the paper towel. Cool, uncovered, for 5 minutes. Gently loosen the edges, remove the cake from the pan, and cool completely on a wire rack. Before serving, top with the coconut-pecan frosting.

YIELD: 6 to 8 servings

> **TIP:** Using a digital scale makes it easy to divide a cake mix in half.

Pies

With this mixture of classic flavors and new favorites, there's a pie for every season and reason. Pies "baked" in the pressure cooker use a cookie crust, but we've also included traditional baked pastry crust recipes for fillings made in the pressure cooker.

Single-Crust Piecrust   90
Double-Crust Piecrust   91
Double Crust Cherry Pie   92
Whole Wheat–Coconut Oil Single Piecrust   94
Caramel Apple Pie   95
Banana Split Pie   97
Coconut Custard Pie   98
Sweet Potato Pie   99
Strawberry Pie   101
Dreamy Orange Pie   102
Vanilla Almond Custard Pie
with Macerated Raspberries   104

◄ Caramel Apple Pie, page 95

▸ PREP TIME: 20 minutes

▸ COOK TIME: 20 minutes

▸ TOTAL TIME: 1 hour,
  10 minutes

SINGLE-CRUST PIECRUST

For us, the perfect piecrust uses a mixture of chilled butter and shortening. You get flakiness from the shortening and rich taste from the butter.

1¼ cups (156 g) all-purpose flour, plus more for rolling the dough

½ teaspoon salt

2 tablespoons (28 g) unsalted butter, chilled

⅓ cup (67 g) shortening, chilled (preferably butter-flavored shortening)

3 tablespoons (45 ml) ice water

In a large bowl, combine the flour and salt. Cut the butter and shortening into small cubes and add them to flour mixture. Use a pastry cutter or two knives to cut the butter and shortening into the flour until it resembles very coarse meal.

One tablespoon (15 ml) at a time, add the water to the dough, mixing it in with a fork. Add just enough water so the dough holds together when you squeeze a handful. (It will still look dry and crumbly.) Form the dough into a round disk and wrap it in plastic wrap. Chill for 30 minutes.

Preheat the oven to 450°F (230°C).

On a well-floured surface, roll the dough into a 12-inch (30 cm) circle that's ⅛ inch (2 mm) thick. Or roll out the dough between sheets of plastic wrap, as described on page 16.

Transfer the crust to a 9-inch (23 cm) pie pan and flute the edges. Prick the bottom of the crust with a fork. Line the crust with a piece of parchment paper and fill the pan with dried beans, uncooked rice, or pie weights. Bake the unfilled piecrust for 15 to 20 minutes until lightly brown.

YIELD: 1 single crust piecrust, 6 to 8 servings when filled

▸ **TIP:** When using a single crust, there is no need to bake the piecrust again after you fill it. Fill the pie with your favorite berry or cherry pie filling, cut, and serve.

DOUBLE-CRUST PIECRUST

This recipe produces a delicate, flaky crust—perfect for making a cutout crust or using small cookie cutters to make a design in the top crust.

2½ cups (313 g) all-purpose flour

1 teaspoon salt

¼ cup (55 g)
unsalted butter, chilled

⅔ cup (133 g) shortening, chilled
(preferably butter-flavored
shortening)

5 to 7 tablespoons (75 to 105 ml)
ice water

In a large bowl, combine the flour and salt. Cut the butter and shortening into small cubes and add them to the flour mixture. Use a pastry cutter or two knives to cut the butter and shortening into the flour until it resembles very coarse meal.

One tablespoon (15 ml) at a time, add the water to the dough, mixing it in with a fork. Add just enough water so the dough holds together when you squeeze a handful. (It will still look dry and crumbly.) Divide the dough in half, form two round disks, and wrap each disk in plastic wrap. Chill for 30 minutes.

Roll out both disks of dough on a floured surface or cut two sheets of plastic wrap and roll the dough out in between them, as described on page 16.

The oven temperature and baking time will differ based on the filling you select for your double crust pie. Refer to the Double-Crust Cherry Pie (page 92) or to your favorite pie recipe for oven temperatures and baking times tailored to your filling.

YIELD: 1 double crust piecrust, 6 to 8 servings when filled

► **TIP:** Rather than flouring a rolling pin and table, you can roll out the piecrust between sheets of plastic wrap. That way, you don't dry out the crust with extra flour, and the plastic wrap keeps the crust from sticking to the counter and makes it easy to transfer to the pie plate.

- PREP TIME: 20 minutes
- COOK TIME: 45 minutes
- TOTAL TIME: 2 hours

DOUBLE-CRUST CHERRY PIE

Homemade cherry pie never goes out of style. Making the filling in your pressure cooker before you fill the crust results in a pie that isn't runny and slices easily every time.

All-purpose flour, for preparing the work surface

Double-Crust Piecrust (page 91)

Cherry Pie Filling (page 150)

1 large egg white, beaten

1 tablespoon (12.5 g) coarse sugar

Vanilla Whipped Cream (page 148) or vanilla ice cream, for serving

Preheat the oven to 425°F (220°C).

On a well-floured surface, roll the bottom crust into a 12-inch (30 cm) circle that's ⅛ inch (2 mm) thick. Transfer the bottom crust to a 9-inch (23 cm) pie pan. Trim the crust even with the edge of the pan. Roll out the top crust in the same manner and set aside.

Spoon the cherry pie filling into the bottom crust. Top the filling with the second crust, seal the edges, and flute them. Brush the top crust with the beaten egg white and sprinkle with the sugar. Cut several slits in the top crust to allow the steam to escape.

Bake for 40 to 45 minutes until the pie is golden brown. (If the edges brown too quickly, cover them with strips of aluminum foil.) Remove from the oven and transfer to a wire rack to cool for at least 1 hour before serving. Serve topped with whipped cream or vanilla ice cream.

YIELD: 6 to 8 servings

> **TIP:** If you prefer, substitute store-bought piecrust for homemade. Just be sure you have enough to make a double crust.

- PREP TIME: 20 minutes
- COOK TIME: 30 minutes
- TOTAL TIME: 1 hour, 20 minutes

WHOLE WHEAT–COCONUT OIL SINGLE PIECRUST

Make your piecrust a little healthier with whole wheat and coconut oil. This is a soft crust that is very easy to work with.

2 cups (240 g) whole-wheat pastry flour, plus more for rolling the dough

½ teaspoon salt

⅔ cup (146 g) solid (not liquid) coconut oil

5 to 6 tablespoons (75 to 90 ml) ice water

In the bowl of a food processor, pulse together the flour and salt until combined. Add the coconut oil and pulse 5 to 6 times. The mixture should resemble wet sand.

Add 5 tablespoons (75 ml) of ice water and pulse 5 to 6 times until the mixture starts to come together. It should stay together when you squeeze it with your hand; if the dough falls apart like sand when you squeeze it, add 1 more tablespoon (15 ml) of water.

Preheat the oven to 350°F (180°).

Scoop the dough onto a lightly floured surface and shape it into a flat disk. Flour the top of the dough. Roll it into a circle just wider than a 9-inch (23 cm) pie plate and about ⅛ inch (2 mm) thick. To prevent the dough from sticking, add extra flour to the bottom and top surfaces as needed. Roll the dough onto the rolling pin to transfer it to the pie plate. Shape the edges as desired. No need to poke holes in the crust.

Bake the piecrust for 25 to 30 minutes. The crust won't brown significantly, so remove it from the oven when it feels crisp and dry to the touch. Place on a wire rack to cool completely before filling.

YIELD: 1 single crust piecrust, 6 to 8 servings when filled

> **TIP:** If you're not using a food processor, mix together the flour and salt, and then cut in the coconut oil with a pastry blender or two knives.

- PREP TIME: 30 minutes
- COOK TIME: 0 minutes
- TOTAL TIME: 30 minutes

CARAMEL APPLE PIE

This pie is 100 percent naturally sweetened with apples, cinnamon, and dates that melt into the filling to create a sweet, caramel-like taste. Great for dessert and healthy enough for breakfast, too!

Naturally Sweetened Caramel Apple Pie Filling (page 151)

Whole Wheat–Coconut Oil Single Piecrust (page 94), baked as directed and cooled

Vanilla Whipped Cream (page 148)

Pour the pie filling into the baked and cooled crust. Serve warm, at room temperature, or cold. Just prior to serving, top with a spoonful of whipped cream.

YIELD: 6 to 8 servings

> ▶ **TIP:** Make it a Dutch apple pie by sprinkling your favorite granola on top.

BANANA SPLIT PIE

This fun summertime pie takes advantage of fabulous, easy-to-make pressure cooker pie fillings and sauces.

FOR GRAHAM CRACKER CRUST

1½ cups (90 g) graham cracker crumbs (about 12 crackers, crushed)

6 tablespoons (84 g) unsalted butter, melted

3 tablespoons (39 g) sugar

FOR FILLING

1 quart vanilla ice cream, softened

2 bananas, sliced

Pineapple Sauce (page 140)

Strawberry Pie Filling (page 154)

Salted Chocolate Dulce de Leche (page 147)

Dulce de Leche (page 146)

Vanilla Whipped Cream (page 148)

Maraschino cherries, for serving

Chopped nuts, for serving

Sprinkles, for serving

Preheat the oven to 350°F (180°C).

To make the graham cracker crust: In a medium bowl, stir together the graham cracker crumbs, butter, and sugar. Press the crust into a 9-inch (23 cm) pie plate and bake for about 10 minutes until lightly browned. Remove from the oven and cool on a wire rack until completely cooled.

To make the filling: Spread the softened ice cream on top of the crust. Freeze until ready to serve.

Serve topped with banana slices, Pineapple Sauce, Strawberry Sauce, Salted Chocolate Dulce de Leche, Dulce de Leche, Whipped Vanilla Cream, cherries, chopped nuts, and sprinkles, as desired.

YIELD: 6 to 8 servings

> **TIP:** Substitute a store-bought graham cracker crust, hot fudge, and caramel ice cream toppings if you prefer.

COCONUT CUSTARD PIE

A coconut lover's delight, this tasty coconut pie has a creamy coconut custard filling and is topped with whipped cream and toasted coconut.

FOR CRUST

Nonstick cooking spray, for preparing the pan

1 cup (60 g) graham cracker crumbs (about 8 crackers, crushed)

3 tablespoons (42 g) unsalted butter, melted

1 tablespoon (13 g) sugar

FOR FILLING

4 large egg yolks

2 tablespoons (26 g) sugar

1 can (14 ounces, or 425 g) sweetened condensed milk

⅓ cup (80 ml) heavy cream

⅓ cup (77 g) sour cream

1½ teaspoons coconut extract

½ teaspoon vanilla extract

1 cup (85 g) sweetened dried shredded coconut

Vanilla Whipped Cream (page 148), for serving

Toasted coconut, for serving

Coat a 7-inch (18 cm) springform pan with nonstick cooking spray.

To make the crust: In a small bowl, stir together the graham cracker crumbs, butter, and sugar. Press the crust evenly in the bottom and no more than 1 inch (2.5 cm) up the side of the prepared pan. Freeze for 10 minutes.

To make the filling: In a large bowl, with a handheld electric mixer, combine the egg yolks and sugar and beat for 2 to 3 minutes on high speed until thick and light yellow. Add the sweetened condensed milk and beat until well incorporated. Add the cream and sour cream, and mix on low speed just until blended. Stir in the coconut extract, vanilla, and shredded coconut. Pour the filling over the crust.

Pour 1 cup (235 ml) of water into the pressure cooking pot and place a trivet in the bottom. Carefully center the filled pan on a sling and lower the pan onto the trivet. Lock the lid in place and turn the pressure release valve to the Sealed position. Select High Pressure and 25 minutes cook time.

When the cook time ends, turn off the pressure cooker. Let the pressure release naturally for 10 minutes, and finish with a quick pressure release. When the valve drops, carefully remove the lid. The top of the pie should be mostly set. If it is still liquid and jiggly, relock the lid and cook at High Pressure for 5 minutes more, followed by another 10-minute natural pressure release.

With the sling, transfer the pan to a wire rack to cool. Cover with plastic wrap and refrigerate for a least 4 hours, or overnight.

Serve topped with the Vanilla Whipped Cream and toasted coconut.

YIELD: 6 to 8 servings

▶ **TIP:** Coconut extract is easy to find in the baking aisle of the grocery store, alongside the vanilla extract.

CHANGE IT UP!

Substitute an Oreo cookie crust and serve with a drizzle of Chocolate Ganache (page 139). If you like Mounds candy bars, you'll love this option.

- ▶ PREP TIME: 10 minutes
- ▶ COOK TIME: 45 minutes
- ▶ TOTAL TIME: 4 hours, or overnight

SWEET POTATO PIE

If you love pumpkin pie, you'll love the fresh sweet potatoes, brown sugar, and gingersnap cookie crust in this sweet potato pie.

FOR CRUST

Nonstick cooking spray, for preparing the pan

1 cup (84 g) crushed gingersnap cookies (about 12 cookies, crushed)

1 tablespoon (13 g) sugar

2 tablespoons (28 g) unsalted butter, melted

FOR FILLING

2 large sweet potatoes (about 2 pounds, or 910 g), peeled, halved lengthwise, and cut into ¼-inch (6 mm) slices

½ cup (120 g) packed light brown sugar

½ teaspoon ground cinnamon

⅛ teaspoon ground nutmeg

1 large egg, beaten

½ cup (120 ml) heavy cream

½ teaspoon vanilla extract

▶ **TIP:** We used Garnet sweet potatoes in this recipe. They have a bright orange flesh and a flavor similar to pumpkin. If you've used a large sweet potato, you may have extra mashed sweet potato; serve this as a side dish with dinner.

Coat a 7-inch (18 cm) springform pan with nonstick cooking spray.

To make the crust: In a small bowl, stir together the gingersnap cookie crumbs, butter, and sugar. Press the crumbs evenly in the bottom and no more than 1 inch (2.5 cm) up the side of the prepared pan. Freeze for 10 minutes.

To make the filling: Pour 1 cup (235 ml) of water into the pressure cooking pot and place a steamer basket in the bottom. Place the sliced sweet potatoes in the steamer basket. Lock the lid in place and turn the pressure release valve to the Sealed position. Select High Pressure and 10 minutes cook time.

When the cook time ends, turn off the pressure cooker and use a quick pressure release. When the valve drops, carefully remove the lid. Transfer the sweet potatoes to a large bowl. Remove the steamer basket from the pot and discard the cooking water.

To the cooked sweet potatoes, add the brown sugar, cinnamon, and nutmeg. With a handheld electric mixer, beat the ingredients on medium speed until smooth. Add the egg, cream, and vanilla. Mix just until blended. Pour the filling into the piecrust. Cover with aluminum foil.

Pour 1 cup (235 ml) of water into the pressure cooking pot and place a trivet in the bottom. Carefully center the filled pan on a sling and lower the pan onto the trivet. Lock the lid in place and turn the pressure release valve to the Sealed position. Select High Pressure and 35 minutes cook time.

When the cook time ends, turn off the pressure cooker. Let the pressure release naturally for 10 minutes, and finish with a quick pressure release. When the valve drops, carefully remove the lid. The middle of the pie should be set. If still liquid and jiggly, relock the lid and cook at High Pressure for 5 minutes more, followed by another 10-minute natural pressure release.

With the sling, transfer the pan to a wire rack to cool. Remove the aluminum foil. When the pie is cooled, cover with plastic wrap and refrigerate for a least 4 hours.

YIELD: 6 to 8 servings

STRAWBERRY PIE

Barbara's daughter's favorite pie is this fresh strawberry pie. It's so easy, you'll want to make it all summer long.

1½ cups (90 g) graham cracker crumbs (about 12 crackers, crushed)

6 tablespoons (84 g) unsalted butter, melted

3 tablespoons (39 g) sugar

Strawberry Pie Filling (page 154)

Vanilla Whipped Cream (page 148)

Preheat the oven to 350°F (180°).

In a medium bowl, stir together the graham cracker crumbs, butter, and sugar. Mix well. Press the crumbs evenly into the bottom and up the side of a 9-inch (23 cm) pie plate. Bake for about 10 minutes until lightly browned. Remove from the oven and transfer to a wire rack to cool completely.

Spoon the strawberry pie filling into the crust. Refrigerate until ready to serve. Top with a dollop of Vanilla Whipped Cream.

YIELD: 6 to 8 servings

▸ **TIP:** If you prefer, substitute a Single Piecrust (page 90) or a ready-made 8-inch (20 cm) graham cracker crust.

DREAMY ORANGE PIE

This pie is bright with orange flavor that pairs perfectly with sweet vanilla cream. Smooth and creamy with a delicious buttery crust.

FOR CRUST

Nonstick cooking spray, for preparing the pan

1 cup (60 g) graham cracker crumbs (about 8 crackers, crushed)

3 tablespoons (42 g) unsalted butter, melted

1 tablespoon (13 g) sugar

FOR FILLING

4 large egg yolks

2 tablespoons (26 g) sugar

1 can (14 fluid ounces, or 425 ml) sweetened condensed milk

⅔ cup (160 g) freshly squeezed orange juice

Zest of 2 medium oranges, plus more for garnishing

Whipped cream, for serving

Coat a 7-inch (18 cm) springform pan with nonstick cooking spray.

To make the crust: In a small bowl, stir together the graham cracker crumbs, butter, and sugar. Press the crumbs evenly in the bottom and no more than 1 inch (2.5 cm) up the side of the prepared pan. Freeze for 10 minutes.

To make the filling: In a large bowl, combine the egg yolks and sugar. With a handheld electric mixer, beat the ingredients for 2 to 3 minutes on high speed until thick and light yellow. Add the sweetened condensed milk and beat until well incorporated. Add the orange juice and orange zest and beat until smooth. Pour the filling over the crust.

Pour 1 cup (235 ml) of water into the pressure cooking pot and place a trivet in the bottom. Carefully center the filled pan on a sling and lower the pan onto the trivet. Lock the lid in place and turn the pressure release valve to the Sealed position. Select High Pressure and 25 minutes cook time.

When the cook time ends, turn off the pressure cooker. Let the pressure release naturally for 10 minutes, and finish with a quick pressure release. When the valve drops, carefully remove the lid. The top of the pie should be mostly set. If it is still liquid and jiggly, relock the lid and cook at High Pressure for 5 minutes more, followed by another 10-minute natural pressure release.

With the sling, transfer the pan to a wire rack to cool. When the pie is cool, cover in plastic wrap and refrigerate for a least 4 hours.

Prior to serving, top with a dollop of Vanilla Whipped Cream and garnish with orange zest.

YIELD: 6 to 8 servings

> **TIP:** For a new spin on this classic vanilla-citrus combo, use lemon, lime, key lime—or even grapefruit instead! Mix and match the citrus to your taste!

- ▶ PREP TIME: 15 minutes
- ▶ COOK TIME: 30 minutes
- ▶ TOTAL TIME: 5 hours, including chilling time

VANILLA ALMOND CUSTARD PIE WITH MACERATED RASPBERRIES

Luscious vanilla and almond custard wrapped in a vanilla crust and dressed with juicy sweet raspberries—if you want a dessert to wow a crowd, this beauty is it!

FOR VANILLA CRUST

Nonstick cooking spray, for preparing the pan

1 cup (80 g) vanilla wafer crumbs (about 22 wafer cookies, crushed)

3 tablespoons (42 g) unsalted butter, melted

FOR FILLING

4 large eggs

⅔ cup (133 g) sugar

¼ teaspoon salt

2 teaspoons vanilla extract

¼ teaspoon almond extract

1½ cups (355 ml) whole milk

1 cup (235 ml) heavy cream

FOR MACERATED RASPBERRIES

1 cup (125 g) fresh raspberries

1 tablespoon (13 g) sugar

Freshly ground nutmeg, for garnishing (optional)

Coat a 7-inch (18 cm) springform pan with nonstick cooking spray.

To make the vanilla crust: In a small bowl, stir together the vanilla wafer crumbs and butter. Press the crust evenly in the bottom and 1 inch (2.5 cm) up the side of the prepared pan. Freeze for 10 minutes.

To make the filling: In a medium bowl, whisk the eggs, sugar, salt, vanilla, and almond extract until smooth. Set aside.

Pour the milk and cream into a medium saucepan and place it over medium-low heat. Heat until bubbles start to form around the edges of the pan. When warm, temper the eggs by pouring ¼ cup (60 ml) of the warm milk mixture into the egg mixture while whisking constantly. Slowly pour the remaining milk mixture into the eggs, whisking until smooth and incorporated. Pour the mixture through a fine-mesh sieve into the crust.

Pour 1 cup (235 ml) of water into the pressure cooking pot and place a trivet in the bottom. Carefully center the filled pan on a sling and lower the pan into the cooking pot. Lock the lid in place and turn the pressure release valve to the Sealed position. Select High Pressure and 30 minutes cook time.

When the cook time ends, turn off the pressure cooker. Let the pressure release naturally for 15 minutes, and finish with a quick pressure release. When the valve drops, carefully remove the lid. The edges should be set and the center slightly jiggly. If not, relock the lid and cook at High Pressure for 5 minutes more, followed by another 10-minute natural pressure release.

Use the sling to transfer the pan to a wire rack to cool. Once the pie is cool, cover and refrigerate for at least 4 hours, or overnight.

To make the Macerated Raspberries: About 30 to 60 minutes before serving, sprinkle the sugar over the raspberries. Cover and refrigerate until the berries have released some of their liquid.

Serve the pie chilled, topped with a spoonful of Macerated Raspberries and a sprinkle of nutmeg, if desired.

YIELD: 6 to 8 servings

▸ **TIP:** To add another layer of wow to this pie, sprinkle it with turbinado sugar and use a kitchen torch to make a crust similar to the Vanilla Bean Crème Brûlée (see page 129) and then top with the Macerated Raspberries.

Cobblers and Fruit Desserts

Fruit desserts brighten any day and can make for a lighter, fresher end to the meal. These desserts are family favorites and perfect for summertime when fresh fruit is in season, or use frozen fruit to brighten a cold winter's night.

▶ Cranberry-Orange Poached Pears   108

▶ No-Sugar-Added Applesauce   110

▶ Banana Boats   111

▶ Strawberry Trifle   112

▶ Peach Cobbler   113

▶ Triple Berry Crisp   115

◀ Triple Berry Crisp, page 115

- ▸ PREP TIME: 10 minutes
- ▸ COOK TIME: 5 minutes
- ▸ TOTAL TIME: 25 minutes

CRANBERRY-ORANGE POACHED PEARS

These poached pears look elegant and beautiful—and they're easy and fast to throw together! Perfect for a healthy weeknight dessert and fancy enough to serve guests.

6 to 8 firm pears, peeled and left whole

2 cups (200 g) fresh cranberries

Zest of 1 large orange

¼ cup (60 ml) pure maple syrup

2 teaspoons vanilla extract

6 to 8 cups (1.4 to 1.9 L) unsweetened apple juice, enough to cover three-fourths of the pears

Vanilla ice cream or Vanilla Whipped Cream (page 148), for serving

Cut the bottoms off the pears so they sit flat when the stem is facing up.

Place the cranberries, orange zest, maple syrup, vanilla, and 2 cups (475 ml) of apple juice into the pressure cooker cooking pot and stir to combine.

Stand the pears inside the cooking pot, stems up, and pour in the remaining apple juice until three-fourths of the pears are covered. Lock the lid in place and turn the pressure release valve to the Sealed position. Select High Pressure and 5 minutes cook time.

When the cook time ends, turn off the pressure cooker. Let the pressure release naturally for 10 minutes, and finish with a quick pressure release. When the valve drops, carefully remove the lid.

With a slotted spoon, carefully remove the pears from the cooking pot and place in individual serving bowls. Spoon some juice from the pot over each pear and serve with a scoop of ice cream or a dollop of Vanilla Whipped Cream.

YIELD: 4 to 6 servings

▸ **TIP:** Don't discard that remaining juice from the poached pears—it is delicious! Pour through a strainer and enjoy hot or cold.

NO-SUGAR-ADDED APPLESAUCE

Homemade applesauce is a sweet fall favorite, but quick and easy enough to make all year.

7 large Gala apples, peeled, cored, and quartered or sliced

3 large Granny Smith apples, peeled, cored, and quartered or sliced

¼ cup (60 ml) unsweetened apple juice

1 teaspoon ground cinnamon (optional)

In the pressure cooking pot, stir together the apples, apple juice, and cinnamon (if using). Lock the lid in place and turn the pressure release valve to the Sealed position. Select High Pressure and 4 minutes cook time.

When the cook time ends, turn off the pressure cooker. Let the pressure release naturally for 5 minutes, and finish with a quick pressure release. When the valve drops, carefully remove the lid. Stir the apples. Use a potato masher or an immersion blender to break up any large chunks and reach the desired consistency. Pour the applesauce into a storage container and cool to room temperature. Refrigerate for up to 10 days or until ready to use.

YIELD: 4 cups (about 980 g)

► **TIP:** Use a blend of sweet and tart apples for the best flavor and texture. However, don't pass up a bargain on apples when you're making applesauce.

BANANA BOATS

These banana boats are the perfect quick dessert that can be customized with each person's favorite flavors. Peanut butter and chocolate chips, strawberries and caramel, honey and cinnamon— the variations are endless!

4 small ripe bananas, unpeeled

Toppings, such as chocolate chips, peanut butter, jam, honey, cinnamon, diced fruit, caramel

Ice cream or Vanilla Whipped Cream (page 148), for serving (optional)

Cut each banana lengthwise through the peel, about ½ inch (1 cm) deep, leaving ½ inch (1 cm) uncut at both ends. Fill the bananas with 1 to 2 tablespoons (weight varies) of your desired toppings (see Tip). Place the filled bananas in a 7 × 3-inch (18 × 7.5 cm) cake pan, stacking them if needed. Make sure the bananas are upright and sturdy so the toppings stay inside the bananas.

Pour 1 cup (235 ml) of water into the pressure cooking pot and place a trivet in the bottom. Carefully center the filled pan on a sling and lower the pan onto the trivet. Lock the lid in place and turn the pressure release valve to the Sealed position. Select High Pressure and 15 minutes cook time.

When the cook time ends, turn off the pressure cooker. Use a quick pressure release. When the valve drops, carefully remove the lid. With the sling, transfer the cake pan to a wire rack. Place the banana boats in individual bowls and serve hot with a scoop of ice cream or Vanilla Whipped Cream, as desired.

YIELD: 4 servings

> **TIP:** When topping the banana boats, add the sweet and melty ingredients before cooking the bananas in the pressure cooker. Save crunchy toppings such as crumbled graham crackers or chopped nuts until just before serving.

STRAWBERRY TRIFLE

A showstopper dessert with layers of pound cake, strawberries, and a light, airy pastry cream.

¾ cup (150 g) sugar

¼ cup (32 g) cornstarch

¼ teaspoon salt

3 large egg yolks

1¾ cups (320 ml) milk

2 tablespoons (28 g) unsalted butter

1 teaspoon vanilla extract

1 teaspoon grated orange zest

1 cup (235 ml) heavy cream

Strawberry Pie Filling (page 154)

1 frozen pound cake (1-pound, or 454 g), thawed, cut into 1-inch (2.5 cm) cubes

Fresh strawberries, for decorating (optional)

In the pressure cooking pot, combine the sugar, cornstarch, and salt. Whisk to combine.

In a medium glass bowl, whisk the egg yolks and milk. Gradually whisk the egg mixture into the sugar mixture. Select Sauté and adjust the heat to low. Cook for about 6 minutes, stirring constantly, until the mixture thickens and just comes to a boil. If the mixture starts to scorch on the bottom, lift the cooking pot away from the heating element, still stirring constantly.

Using hot pads or silicone mitts, transfer the cooking pot to a heat-resistant surface. Whisk in the butter, vanilla, and orange zest. Transfer the custard to a clean medium bowl. Place plastic wrap directly on the surface of the warm filling to prevent a film from forming. Refrigerate for at least 2 hours.

In a separate medium bowl, using a handheld electric mixer, whip the cream on medium speed until soft peaks form. Fold the whipped cream into the chilled pastry cream.

Place half the cake cubes in a 3-quart (2.8 L) trifle dish or glass bowl. Layer half the strawberry pie filling on top of the cake cubes. Top the strawberries with a layer of custard. Repeat the layers. Finish with fresh berries, if desired. Refrigerate for 2 hours before serving.

YIELD: 8 to 10 servings

▶ **TIP:** If your pressure cooker doesn't allow you to adjust the heat setting to low, keep a close watch on the pastry cream, or make it on the stovetop. You can also substitute packaged vanilla pudding made according to package directions for the pastry cream and layer it with the strawberry pie filling.

PEACH COBBLER

Fluffy moist cake with sweet, syrupy peaches topped with a big scoop of melty vanilla ice cream—this peach cobbler will take you back to Dutch oven get-togethers with family and friends.

FOR PEACHES

Nonstick cooking spray, for preparing the pan

3 cups (510 g) fresh sliced (1-inch, or 2.5 cm, wedges) peaches

2 tablespoons (26 g) sugar

1 tablespoon (8 g) cornstarch

FOR BATTER

1 box (16 ounces, or 454 g) yellow cake mix

1 teaspoon baking powder

½ cup (1 stick, or 112 g) unsalted butter, melted

1¼ cups (295 ml) water

Ground cinnamon, for topping

Sugar, for topping

Vanilla ice cream, for serving

To make the peaches: Coat a 7 × 3-inch (18 × 7.5 cm) cake pan with nonstick cooking spray. Place the peaches inside and sprinkle with the sugar and cornstarch. Toss lightly to coat.

To make the batter: In a large bowl, whisk together the cake mix and baking powder. Add the butter and water. Whisk for 1 minute to combine well. Pour the batter evenly over the peaches.

Pour 1 cup (235 ml) of water into the pressure cooking pot and place a trivet in the bottom. Carefully center the filled pan on a sling and lower the pan onto the trivet. Lock the lid in place and turn the pressure release valve to the Sealed position. Select High Pressure and 40 minutes cook time.

When the cook time ends, turn off the pressure cooker. Let the pressure release naturally for 10 minutes, and finish with a quick pressure release. When the valve drops, carefully remove the lid. With the sling, transfer the pan to a sheet pan.

Preheat the broiler.

Sprinkle the cobbler generously with cinnamon and sugar. Place the cobbler under the broiler for 1 to 2 minutes until the sugar caramelizes. Watch closely—it can burn quickly. Remove from the oven and transfer the pan to a cooling rack. Cool for 10 minutes. Serve topped with a scoop of vanilla ice cream.

YIELD: 6 to 8 servings

> **TIP:** To enjoy this cobbler year-round, when fresh peaches are not in season, use 3 cups (750 g) thawed frozen peaches or drained canned peaches instead.

- PREP TIME: 5 minutes
- COOK TIME: 20 minutes
- TOTAL TIME: 40 minutes

TRIPLE BERRY CRISP

Sweet, tart berries topped with a buttery, cinnamon, brown sugar, oat, and almond crumble—a simply perfect dessert any time of year!

Nonstick cooking spray, for preparing the pan

Triple Berry Pie Filling (page 155)

⅔ cup (150 g) packed light brown sugar

½ cup (63 g) all-purpose flour

½ cup (78 g) old-fashioned rolled oats (not quick cooking)

⅓ cup (40 g) sliced almonds

¼ teaspoon ground cinnamon

⅛ teaspoon salt

⅓ cup (75 g) unsalted butter, melted

Vanilla ice cream (optional)

Coat a 7 × 3-inch (18 × 7.5 cm) cake pan with nonstick cooking spray. Pour the pie filling into the prepared pan.

In a large bowl, stir together the brown sugar, flour, oats, almonds, cinnamon, and salt. Add the butter and mix with a fork until the mixture resembles crumbly wet sand. Sprinkle the mixture evenly on top of the pie filling. Cover the pan with aluminum foil.

Pour 1 cup (235 ml) of water into the pressure cooking pot and place a trivet in the bottom. Carefully center the filled pan on a sling and lower the pan onto the trivet. Lock the lid in place and turn the pressure release valve to the Sealed position. Select High Pressure and 20 minutes cook time.

When the cook time ends, turn off the pressure cooker. Let the pressure release naturally for 10 minutes, and finish with a quick pressure release. When the valve drops, carefully remove the lid.

With the sling, transfer the pan to a wire rack and remove the foil. If you want a browner top, put the dish under a preheated broiler for a few minutes until brown. Watch it carefully to prevent burning. Serve piping hot with a scoop of vanilla ice cream, if desired.

YIELD: 6 servings

> **TIP:** You can also mix the crumble topping in a zip-top bag.

Custards and Puddings

Thick and smooth, rich and creamy, these classic desserts come together in a flash and will satisfy your sweet tooth on demand.

▶ **Berry Cherry Pudding Cake** 118

▶ **Lemon Blueberry Bread Pudding** 119

▶ **S'more Bread Pudding** 121

▶ **Chocolate Tapioca Pudding** 122

▶ **Fluffy Minute Tapioca Pudding** 123

▶ **White Chocolate–Lime Rice Pudding** 124

▶ **Vanilla Bean Rice Pudding** 126

▶ **Caramel Pots de Crème** 127

▶ **Coconut Flan** 128

▶ **Vanilla Bean Crème Brûlée** 129

◀ White Chocolate-Lime Rice Pudding, page 126

BERRY CHERRY PUDDING CAKE

This sweet pudding-like fruit is covered with vanilla cake and topped with a scoop of ice cream to cool it all down. Serve hot so the ice cream melts into the sweet-tart fruit!

FOR FRUIT

Nonstick cooking spray, for preparing the pan

3 cups (420 g) frozen mixed berries and cherries

⅓ cup (67 g) sugar

1 tablespoon (8 g) cornstarch

FOR BATTER

1 cup (125 g) all-purpose flour

⅓ cup (67 g) sugar

2 teaspoons baking powder

1 teaspoon ground cinnamon

¼ teaspoon salt

½ cup (120 ml) milk

2 tablespoons (28 g) unsalted butter, melted

1 teaspoon vanilla extract

¾ cup (175 ml) boiling water

Vanilla ice cream, for serving

To make the fruit: Coat a 7 × 3-inch (18 × 7.5 cm) cake pan with nonstick cooking spray. Place the berries and cherries inside the pan and sprinkle them with the sugar followed by the cornstarch.

To make the batter: In a medium bowl, whisk the flour, sugar, baking powder, cinnamon, and salt.

In a large bowl, stir together the milk, butter, and vanilla until blended. Add the dry ingredients and mix just until blended. Spoon the batter evenly over the berries, and gently pour the boiling water over the batter.

Pour 1 cup (235 ml) of water into the pressure cooking pot and place a trivet in the bottom. Carefully center the filled pan on a sling and lower the pan onto the trivet. Lock the lid in place and turn the pressure release valve to the Sealed position. Select High Pressure and 20 minutes cook time.

When the cook time ends, turn off the pressure cooker. Use a quick pressure release. When the valve drops, carefully remove the lid. With the sling, transfer the cake pan to a wire rack. Cool for 10 minutes. Serve hot with a scoop of vanilla ice cream.

YIELD: 6 to 8 servings

> **TIP:** This recipe is very versatile. Use any combination of fresh or frozen fruit you like! Just remember to pit fresh fruits, such as cherries, before adding them to the pan.

- ▶ PREP TIME: 5 minutes
- ▶ COOK TIME: 30 minutes
- ▶ TOTAL TIME: 50 minutes

LEMON BLUEBERRY BREAD PUDDING

A decadently delicious bread pudding made with croissants and heavy cream. The lemon and blueberries give it a bright, tart flavor that's perfectly complemented by the rich and creamy Crème Anglaise.

Unsalted butter, for preparing the pan

3 large eggs

½ cup (100 g) sugar

1 teaspoon vanilla extract

Zest of 1 lemon

2 cups (475 ml) heavy cream

3 large croissants, torn into bite-size pieces

3 cups (135 g) cubed white bread (from about 6 slices)

⅓ cup (50 g) fresh blueberries (see Tip)

Crème Anglaise (page 143), for serving (optional)

Butter a 7 × 3-inch (18 × 7.5 cm) cake pan and set aside.

In a large bowl, whisk the eggs, sugar, vanilla, and lemon zest to combine. Whisk in the heavy cream. Gently stir in the croissants, bread cubes, and blueberries. Pour the batter into the prepared pan.

Pour 1 cup (235 ml) of water into the pressure cooking pot and place a trivet in the bottom. Carefully center the pan on a sling and lower the pan onto the trivet. Lock the lid in place and turn the pressure release valve to the Sealed position. Select High Pressure and 30 minutes cook time.

When the cook time ends, turn off the pressure cooker. Let the pressure release naturally for 10 minutes, and finish with a quick pressure release. When the valve drops, carefully remove the lid. With the sling, transfer the pan to a wire rack to cool for at least 15 minutes before serving.

To serve, slice into wedges and drizzle with Crème Anglaise, if desired

YIELD: 6 to 8 servings

> ▶ **TIP:** You can use frozen blueberries in this recipe. If you do, don't thaw the berries before adding them to the batter, and increase the cook time to 35 minutes.

- PREP TIME: 15 minutes
- COOK TIME: 35 minutes
- TOTAL TIME: 60 minutes

S'MORE BREAD PUDDING

Sweet marshmallow custard, chocolate chips, and crushed graham crackers give you all the classic flavors of a s'more in a soft, gooey slice of warm bread pudding. You may love this even more than the classic campfire version!

FOR MARSHMALLOW GLAZE

½ cup (52 g) marshmallow cream

2 teaspoons milk

½ teaspoon vanilla extract

FOR BREAD PUDDING

Butter, for preparing the pan

3 large eggs

¼ cup (50 g) sugar

1 cup (235 ml) heavy cream

1 cup (104 g) marshmallow cream

1 teaspoon vanilla extract

6 cups (822 g) cubed brioche or French bread

½ cup (88 g) semisweet chocolate chips

½ cup (25 g) mini marshmallows

½ cup (30 g) coarsely crushed graham crackers

To make the marshmallow glaze: Combine the marshmallow cream, milk, and vanilla in a small bowl and whisk until smooth. Refrigerate until ready to use.

To make the bread pudding: Grease a 7 × 3-inch (18 × 7.5 cm) cake pan with butter.

In a large bowl, using a handheld electric mixer, beat the eggs, sugar, cream, marshmallow cream, and vanilla until smooth. (Don't worry if the marshmallow cream isn't fully incorporated; it will melt into the batter as it cooks.) Gently stir in the bread. Scatter the top with chocolate chips and barely fold them in. Pour into the prepared pan.

Pour 1 cup (235 ml) of water into the pressure cooking pot and place a trivet in the bottom. Carefully center the filled pan on a sling and lower the pan into the cooking pot. Lock the lid in place and turn the pressure release valve to the Sealed position. Select High Pressure and 35 minutes cook time.

When the cook time ends, turn off the pressure cooker. Let the pressure release naturally for 10 minutes, and finish with a quick pressure release. When the valve drops, carefully remove the lid. Use the sling to remove the pan from the cooking pot.

Preheat the broiler.

Scatter the marshmallows over the bread pudding and place under the broiler to brown for 2 to 3 minutes. Watch closely as the marshmallows cook quickly.

Cool for at least 15 minutes more before serving. To serve, slice into wedges, drizzle with marshmallow glaze, and sprinkle with crushed graham crackers.

YIELD: 6 to 8 servings

> **TIP:** If you have large marshmallows on hand, use kitchen shears to quickly cut them into quarters to scatter over the top of the bread pudding.

CHOCOLATE TAPIOCA PUDDING

An old-fashioned pudding with a chocolate twist. Use a nonstick pressure cooking pot when making this recipe.

½ cup (75 g) small-pearl tapioca, such as Reese's (see Tip)

1½ cups (355 ml) water

½ cup (100 g) sugar

¼ teaspoon salt

2 large egg yolks

½ cup (117 ml) whole milk

⅓ cup (58 g) semisweet chocolate chips

½ teaspoon vanilla extract

Vanilla Whipped Cream (page 148)

In a nonstick pressure cooking pot, stir together the tapioca and water. Lock the lid in place and turn the pressure release valve to the Sealed position. Select High Pressure and 6 minutes cook time.

When the cook time ends, turn off the pressure cooker. Let the pressure release naturally for 10 minutes, and finish with a quick pressure release. When the valve drops, carefully remove the lid. Whisk the sugar and salt into the tapioca.

In a small mixing bowl, whisk together the egg yolks and milk. Pour the egg mixture through a fine-mesh strainer into the cooking pot. Select Sauté. Cook, stirring constantly, until the mixture just starts to boil. Turn off the pressure cooker. Using hot pads or silicone mitts, transfer the cooking pot to a heat-resistant surface and stir in the chocolate chips and vanilla.

Cool the tapioca to room temperature, stirring occasionally. (The pudding will thicken as it cools.) Pour into serving dishes and chill. Serve topped with the Vanilla Whipped Cream.

YIELD: 4 servings

> **TIP:** Do not use minute tapioca in this recipe. Use a small pearl tapioca with package directions that instruct you to do an overnight soak. If the package directions don't recommend an overnight soak, reduce the cook time on this recipe by a few minutes.

FLUFFY MINUTE TAPIOCA PUDDING

We're often asked if it's possible to cook minute tapioca in the pressure cooker. Since minute tapioca cooks so quickly, it doesn't need to be pressure cooked, but if you like you can cook it using the Sauté button.

3 cups (705 ml) whole milk, divided (see Tip)

2 large eggs, separated

½ cup (96 g) minute tapioca

½ cup (100 g) sugar, divided

¼ teaspoon salt

½ teaspoon vanilla extract

In the pressure cooking pot whisk the milk and egg yolks to combine. Stir in the tapioca, ¼ cup (50 g) of sugar, and the salt. Select Sauté and cook, stirring constantly, until the mixture comes to a full boil. Using hot pads or silicone mitts, transfer the cooking pot to a heat-resistant surface and stir in the vanilla.

In a small bowl, with a handheld electric mixer, beat the egg whites on high speed until foamy. Gradually beat in the remaining ¼ cup (50 g) of sugar until soft peaks form. Gently fold the beaten whites into the pudding. Pour the pudding into serving dishes and serve warm, or refrigerate, covered, for up to 2 days.

YIELD: 6 to 8 servings

> **TIP:** While you might be tempted to use a lower-fat milk, the consistency of this tapioca really needs the richness of whole milk.

WHITE CHOCOLATE–LIME RICE PUDDING

Sweet white chocolate and a hint of fresh lime give this rice pudding a unique twist. Top it with fresh sugared fruit for a special treat.

1 cup (180 g) arborio rice

1½ cups (353 ml) water

¼ teaspoon salt

Zest of 1 lime

Juice of ½ of a lime (reserve the other half for the sugared fruit)

2 cups (475 ml) whole milk, divided, plus more as needed

½ cup (100 g) sugar

3 ounces (85 g) white chocolate, chopped or grated

2 large eggs

2 teaspoons vanilla extract

Tropical Sugared Fruit (page 149) for serving (optional)

Lime wedges, for serving (optional)

In the pressure cooking pot, combine the rice, water, salt, lime zest, and lime juice. Lock the lid in place and turn the pressure release valve to the Sealed position. Select High Pressure and 3 minutes cook time.

When the cook time ends, turn off the pressure cooker. Let the pressure release naturally for 10 minutes, and finish with a quick pressure release. When the valve drops, carefully remove the lid.

Add 1½ cups (360 ml) of the milk, the sugar, and the white chocolate. Stir to combine.

In a small bowl, whisk the eggs with the remaining ½ cup (120 ml) of milk and the vanilla. Pour through a fine-mesh strainer into the cooking pot. Select Sauté and cook, stirring constantly, until the mixture starts to boil. Turn off the pressure cooker and, with hot pads or silicone mitts, remove the inner cooking pot and place it on a heat-resistant surface.

The pudding will thicken as it cools. Serve warm or scoop into serving dishes and chill. The rice will continue to absorb liquid as it cools. Stir in additional milk until your desired consistency is achieved.

Serve topped with Tropical Sugared Fruit and an extra squeeze of lime juice, if desired.

YIELD: 6 to 8 servings

> **TIP:** For a dark chocolate rice pudding, omit the lime and white chocolate and substitute chopped bittersweet chocolate. Top with Macerated Strawberries (page 85).

VANILLA BEAN RICE PUDDING

Rice pudding has never been faster or easier to make than with this rich-and-creamy recipe. The intense vanilla bean flavor makes this pudding anything but ordinary!

1 cup (180 g) arborio rice

1½ cups (353 ml) water

¼ teaspoon salt

2 cups (475 ml) whole milk, divided, plus more as needed (see Tip)

½ cup (100 g) sugar

2 large eggs

1 teaspoon vanilla bean paste (see Tip)

Vanilla Whipped Cream (page 148), for serving

Ground cinnamon or nutmeg, for sprinkling

In the pressure cooking pot, combine the rice, water, and salt. Lock the lid in place and turn the pressure release valve to the Sealed position. Select High Pressure and 3 minutes cook time.

When the cook time ends, turn off the pressure cooker. Let the pressure release naturally for 10 minutes, and finish with a quick pressure release. When the valve drops, carefully remove the lid. Stir in 1½ cups (360 ml) of milk and the sugar.

In a small bowl, whisk the eggs with the remaining ½ cup (120 ml) of milk and the vanilla. Pour the egg mixture through a fine-mesh strainer into the cooking pot. Select Sauté and cook, stirring constantly, until the mixture starts to boil. Turn off the pressure cooker. The pudding will thicken as it cools; stir in more milk until your desired consistency is achieved.

Serve warm or pour into serving dishes and chill. Top with the whipped cream and sprinkle with cinnamon or nutmeg.

YIELD: 8 servings

▶ **TIP:** For a richer, creamier rice pudding, use 1 cup (235 ml) whole milk and 1 cup (235 ml) heavy cream. If you don't have vanilla bean paste, substitute 1 vanilla bean or 1 teaspoon vanilla extract. To use a vanilla bean, warm the milk in a small saucepan over medium-low heat. (Do not boil!) With a sharp knife, split the vanilla bean in half horizontally. Scrape the seeds inside the vanilla bean into the warmed milk.

- ▶ PREP TIME: 10 minutes
- ▶ COOK TIME: 6 minutes
- ▶ TOTAL TIME: 30 minutes, plus chilling time

CARAMEL POTS DE CRÈME

Don't be intimidated by the fancy name—it couldn't be easier to make this tasty treat in the pressure cooker! Sweet creamy caramel pudding with a pinch of salt that makes it extra special.

1 cup (235 ml) heavy cream

1 cup (235 ml) half-and-half

5 large egg yolks

3 tablespoons (45 g) brown sugar

¼ teaspoon salt

1 cup (235 ml) jarred butterscotch caramel, warmed until thin enough to drizzle

Vanilla Whipped Cream (page 148), for serving

Flaky sea salt, for garnishing

In a saucepan over medium heat, combine the cream and half-and-half. Bring to a light simmer, stirring occasionally.

In a large bowl, whisk the egg yolks, brown sugar, and salt. Slowly whisk in the hot cream mixture. Whisk in the butterscotch caramel. Divide the batter among six (6-ounce, or 175 ml) ramekins and cover each with aluminum foil.

Add 1 cup (235 ml) of water to the pressure cooking pot and place a trivet in the bottom. Place three ramekins on the trivet and place a second trivet on top. Stack the remaining three ramekins on top of the second trivet. Lock the lid in place and turn the pressure release valve to the Sealed position. Select High Pressure and 6 minutes cook time.

When the cook time ends, turn off the pressure cooker. Let the pressure release naturally for 15 minutes, and finish with a quick pressure release. When the valve drops, carefully remove the lid.

Transfer the ramekins to a wire rack, remove the aluminum foil, and cool to room temperature. Cover with plastic wrap and refrigerate for at least 4 hours, or overnight.

Serve cold with an extra drizzle of caramel, a dollop of Vanilla Whipped Cream, and a pinch of flaky sea salt.

YIELD: 6 servings

> ▶ **TIP:** Instead of store-bought butterscotch caramel, make your own homemade Dulce de Leche (page 146) or Salted Chocolate Dulce de Leche (page 147).

COCONUT FLAN

Flan is a popular creamy custard dessert that is served inverted on a platter, revealing a sweet caramel topping. Serve chilled and use a spoon to scoop up the luscious caramel with each bite.

Nonstick cooking spray, for preparing the pan

⅓ cup (80 ml) jarred caramel sauce or warmed Dulce de Leche (page 146)

4 large eggs

2 cans (14 fluid ounces, or 425 ml, each) sweetened condensed milk

1 can (14 fluid ounces, or 425 ml, each) unsweetened coconut milk

1 tablespoon (15 ml) vanilla extract

¼ teaspoon salt

⅓ cup (28 g) shredded sweetened coconut, toasted

Coat a half-size Bundt pan with nonstick cooking spray.

Pour the caramel sauce into the pan and turn to coat the bottom and sides. Set aside.

In a large bowl, whisk together the eggs. Add the condensed milk, coconut milk, vanilla, and salt and whisk until smooth. Pour the mixture into the prepared Bundt pan.

Pour 1 cup (235 ml) of water into the pressure cooking pot and place a trivet in the bottom. Carefully center the filled pan on a sling and lower the pan into the cooking pot. Lock the lid in place and turn the pressure release valve to the sealed position. Select High Pressure and 30 minutes cook time.

When the cook time ends, turn off the pressure cooker. Let the pressure release naturally for 15 minutes, and finish with a quick pressure release. When the valve drops, carefully remove the lid.

Use the sling to transfer the pan to a wire rack to cool, uncovered. Once cool, cover with plastic wrap and refrigerate for 4 hours, or overnight.

To serve, turn the flan onto a platter with edges to contain the caramel sauce. Sprinkle with toasted coconut and serve.

YIELD: 6 to 8 servings

> **TIP:** Plan ahead! This flan needs to be well chilled to achieve its famous creamy, custard texture.

- ▶ PREP TIME: 20 minutes
- ▶ COOK TIME: 6 minutes
- ▶ TOTAL TIME: 45 minutes,
  plus chilling time

VANILLA BEAN CRÈME BRÛLÉE

A pressure cooker is the perfect moist environment to create a dreamy crème brûlée. Using a vanilla bean makes the vanilla flavor even more intense and memorable.

2 cups (475 ml) heavy cream

⅓ cup (67 g) granulated sugar

Pinch salt

1 vanilla bean, split, seeds scraped out

6 large egg yolks

6 tablespoons (78 g) superfine sugar or turbinado sugar, divided

In a medium saucepan over medium heat, combine the cream, sugar, salt, vanilla bean pod, and vanilla seeds. Bring the mixture to a simmer. Remove from the heat and let cool for 15 minutes.

In a large bowl, whisk together the eggs yolks. Add ¼ cup (60 ml) of the warm cream mixture and whisk to temper the eggs. Continue whisking and pour the remaining warm cream into the bowl. Stir until combined. Pour the mixture through a fine-mesh strainer into a large container with a pour spout. Divide the mixture among six (6-ounce, or 175 ml) ramekins and cover each with aluminum foil.

Add 1 cup (235 ml) of water to the pressure cooking pot and place a trivet in the bottom. Place three ramekins on the trivet and place a second trivet on top. Stack the remaining three ramekins on top of the second trivet. Lock the lid in place and turn the pressure release valve to the Sealed position. Select High Pressure and 6 minutes cook time.

When the cook time ends, turn off the pressure cooker. Let the pressure release naturally for 10 minutes, and finish with a quick pressure release. When the valve drops, carefully remove the lid.

Transfer the ramekins to a wire rack to cool, uncovered, to room temperature. Cover with plastic wrap and refrigerate for at least 4 hours, or up to 2 days.

When ready to serve, sprinkle 1 tablespoon (13 g) of sugar to cover the entire surface of each custard. Working one at a time, moving in a circular motion, hold a kitchen torch about 2 inches (5 cm) above the surface of each custard to melt the sugar and form a crisp, caramelized topping. Serve immediately.

YIELD: 6 servings

▶ **TIP:** The sugar can be caramelized without a kitchen torch by placing the ramekins under a preheated broiler for 1 to 2 minutes. Watch closely, they will brown quickly.

Sauces, Fillings, and Toppings

We've put all the compotes, sauces, syrups, fillings, and frostings in one easy-to-use section. Feel free to mix and match your favorite sauces with the different recipes throughout the cookbook.

- Berry Cherry Chia Compote — 132
- Cinnamon Vanilla Coconut Syrup — 135
- Dark Chocolate Syrup — 136
- Strawberry Vanilla Honey Syrup — 138
- Chocolate Ganache — 139
- Pineapple Sauce — 140
- Raspberry-Orange Yogurt Sauce — 142
- Crème Anglaise — 143
- Coconut-Pecan Frosting — 144
- Cream Cheese Yogurt Frosting — 145
- Dulce de Leche — 146
- Salted Chocolate Dulce de Leche — 147
- Vanilla Whipped Cream — 148
- Tropical Sugared Fruit — 149
- Cherry Pie Filling — 150
- Naturally Sweetened Caramel Apple Pie Filling — 151
- Lemon Curd — 153
- Strawberry Pie Filling — 154
- Triple Berry Pie Filling — 155

BERRY CHERRY CHIA COMPOTE

This compote is a perfect mix of sweet and tart. The secret ingredient? Chia seeds, which thicken the compote and add another layer of nutrition.

4 cups (560 g) mixed frozen berries and cherries

⅓ cup (80 ml) pure maple syrup

Juice of ½ of a lemon

⅓ cup (40 g) chia seeds

In the pressure cooking pot, combine the frozen fruit, maple syrup, and lemon juice. Stir to mix. Lock the lid in place and turn the pressure release valve to the Sealed position. Select High Pressure and 2 minutes cook time.

When the cook time ends, turn off the pressure cooker. Let the pressure release naturally for 10 minutes, and finish with a quick pressure release. When the valve drops, carefully remove the lid.

Immediately stir in the chia seeds, stirring quickly to avoid clumping. Cover the pot with the lid and let sit for 20 minutes to thicken. Serve hot or cold. The compote will thicken further when chilled. Keep refrigerated in an airtight container for up to 1 week, or frozen for up to 2 months.

YIELD: 2 cups (about 650 g)

► **TIP:** Chia seeds are used to thicken the compote. If you prefer to omit them, you can still thicken the compote. After pressure cooking, make a slurry of 2 tablespoons (16 g) cornstarch whisked with 2 tablespoons (30 ml) cold water. Select Sauté. Pour the cornstarch mixture into the compote and cook, stirring, until it thickens.

- PREP TIME: 1 minute
- COOK TIME: 10 minutes
- TOTAL TIME: 20 minutes

CINNAMON VANILLA COCONUT SYRUP

This syrup is absolutely delicious, and it works on so many things! Try it for breakfast on pancakes, waffles, and yogurt, or for dessert over ice cream and cake.

1 can (14 fluid ounces, or 425 ml) light unsweetened coconut milk (see Tip)

½ cup (120 ml) pure maple syrup

3 cinnamon sticks

½ of a vanilla bean, split, or 2 teaspoons pure vanilla extract

Pinch kosher salt

In the pressure cooking pot, combine the coconut milk, maple syrup, cinnamon sticks, vanilla bean, and salt. Whisk until blended. Lock the lid in place and turn the pressure release valve to the Sealed position. Select High Pressure and 10 minutes cook time.

When the cook time ends, turn off the pressure cooker. Use a quick pressure release. When the valve drops, carefully remove the lid.

Select Sauté. Simmer the syrup for 5 to 10 minutes, stirring often, until it thickens slightly. Carefully pour the syrup into an 8-ounce (235 ml) Mason jar and top with a Mason jar pour cap. Use immediately or refrigerate for up to 2 weeks. Shake well before each use.

YIELD: About 1 cup (235 ml)

> **TIP:** Be sure to use light coconut milk in this recipe. Light coconut milk has a higher water content and will keep the syrup from solidifying when chilled.

- ► PREP TIME: 3 minutes
- ► COOK TIME: 10 minutes
- ► TOTAL TIME: 20 minutes

DARK CHOCOLATE SYRUP

This incredibly rich, chocolatey syrup is made with light coconut milk and sweetened with pure maple syrup, making it the perfect accent for anything and everything you put it on!

1 can (14 fluid ounces, or 425 ml) light unsweetened coconut milk

½ cup (120 ml) pure maple syrup

2 tablespoons (10 g) dark 100% cocoa powder

1 tablespoon (15 ml) vanilla extract

Pinch kosher salt

In the pressure cooking pot, combine the coconut milk, maple syrup, cocoa powder, vanilla, and salt. Whisk until the cocoa powder is well combined in the liquid. Lock the lid in place and turn the pressure release valve to the Sealed position. Select High Pressure and 10 minutes cook time.

When the cook time ends, turn off the pressure cooker. Use a quick pressure release. When the valve drops, carefully remove the lid.

Select Sauté and simmer the sauce for 5 to 10 minutes, stirring often until thickened slightly. Pour the syrup through a fine-mesh sieve into a Mason jar and top with a Mason jar pour cap. Keep refrigerated for up to 2 weeks. The syrup will thicken as it cools. Shake well before each use.

YIELD: About 1 cup (235 ml)

► **TIP:** If you don't have dark cocoa powder, substitute any cocoa powder you have on hand; the result will be a milder chocolate flavor.

STRAWBERRY VANILLA HONEY SYRUP

Flavored honey can be so pricey—luckily, you can make your own in your pressure cooker! This red-tinted strawberry vanilla honey syrup is beautifully flavored and perfect for fresh, warm biscuits.

½ cup (85 g) frozen sliced strawberries (see Tip)

1 teaspoon vanilla extract or ¼ vanilla bean, slit, halved widthwise

½ cup (170 g) honey

Place the strawberries, vanilla, and honey into a pint-size (480 ml) Mason jar. Stack two round coffee filters together and trim them so they over hang the jar by about 1 inch (2.5 cm). (This keeps excess moisture out of the honey.) Place the filters on top of the jar's opening and screw the ring on tightly (no flat lid needed).

Pour 1 cup (235 ml) of water into the pressure cooking pot and place a trivet in the bottom. Put the jar on the trivet. Lock the lid in place and turn the pressure release valve to the Sealed position. Select High Pressure and 30 minutes cook time.

When the cook time ends, turn off the pressure cooker. Let the pressure release naturally. When the valve drops, carefully remove the lid.

With canning jar lifter tongs, carefully remove the Mason jar. Using hot pads or silicone mitts, remove the lid and vigorously stir the honey to infuse it with maximum flavor. Pour the honey through a small fine-mesh sieve placed over a half-pint (235 ml) Mason jar. Discard the add-ins. Top the Mason jar with a Mason jar pour cap.

Refrigerate the honey. If it becomes too thick, place the jar inside a bowl of hot water to warm it and make it pourable.

YIELD: ¾ cup (180 ml)

> **TIP:** Use the strawberries straight from the freezer—no thawing necessary! You need the juices the frozen strawberries release as they thaw inside the cooking pot to flavor the honey.

- ▶ PREP TIME: 5 minutes
- ▶ COOK TIME: 1 minute
- ▶ TOTAL TIME: 30 minutes

CHOCOLATE GANACHE

The perfect chocolate icing for chocolate cake, cheesecakes, and even fresh berries. The heavy cream keeps the chocolate from setting up too much, so it's always soft, rich, and creamy!

6 ounces (170 g) milk chocolate, finely chopped

⅓ cup (80 ml) heavy cream

Place the chopped chocolate in a microwave-safe glass bowl.

In a small, microwave-safe dish, heat the cream in the microwave just until it starts to bubble around the edges. Pour the cream over the chocolate and let rest for 2 minutes. Stir until smooth. If necessary, reheat in the microwave on medium power to melt the remaining chocolate.

Cool until the ganache is thickened but still thin enough to drip down the sides of the cheesecake or cake.

YIELD: 1 cup (235 ml)

> ▶ **TIP:** If you're in a hurry, cool the ganache in the refrigerator, but check it frequently because it goes from too thin to too thick very quickly.

PINEAPPLE SAUCE

This is a quick, easy-to-make sauce that adds a bright yellow color and sweet pineapple flavor to any dessert.

1 can (8 ounces, or 225 g) crushed pineapple in juice

½ cup (100 g) sugar

Pinch table salt

Place a fine-mesh strainer over the pressure cooking pot. Drain the pineapple through the strainer, allowing the juice to collect inside the pot. Press on the pineapple to squeeze out additional juice. Set the crushed pineapple solids aside.

On your pressure cooker, select Sauté. Boil the pineapple liquid for 2 to 3 minutes until it is reduced by half, (about 2 tablespoons, or 30 ml). Stir in the crushed pineapple solids, the sugar, and salt. Simmer until the sugar dissolves and the mixture is syrupy, about 5 minutes. Remove from the heat.

Cool to room temperature, cover, and refrigerate until ready to serve.

YIELD: about 1 cup (235 ml)

> **TIP:** Double this recipe if you like to load up your cheesecake with topping.

- PREP TIME: 5 minutes
- COOK TIME: 0 minutes
- TOTAL TIME: 5 minutes

RASPBERRY-ORANGE YOGURT SAUCE

This naturally sweetened yogurt sauce makes any breakfast food a great start to your day—try it with the Honey Orange Poppy Seed Breakfast Cake (page 134).

½ cup (125 g) plain Greek yogurt

¼ cup (80 g) raspberry jam

Juice of 1 orange

In a small bowl, whisk together the yogurt, raspberry jam, and orange juice until smooth. If your raspberry jam is more jelly-like, warm it in the microwave just until it's loose enough to mix into the yogurt. Serve at room temperature or refrigerate until ready to serve. This sauce can be made up to 3 days in advance.

YIELD: ¾ cup (175 ml)

> **TIP:** This yogurt sauce also makes a tasty fruit dip!

CRÈME ANGLAISE

Crème anglaise is a silky smooth vanilla custard sauce. It's easy to make and makes any dessert special.

¾ cup (175 ml) heavy cream

¼ cup (60 ml) milk

2 large egg yolks

⅓ cup (67 g) sugar

1 teaspoon vanilla bean paste or extract

In a small saucepan over medium heat, whisk the cream and milk. Cook until the mixture just begins to boil. Remove from the heat.

In a medium bowl, whisk together the egg yolks and sugar. Whisk in half of the hot milk mixture. Add the egg mixture to the saucepan and cook over medium heat, stirring constantly, until the sauce comes to a boil. Reduce the heat to low and simmer for about 2 minutes until the sauce thickens slightly. Remove from the heat and stir in the vanilla.

YIELD: 1 cup (235 ml)

> **TIP:** You can make this in your pressure cooker if your pressure cooker has a Sauté setting that will let you adjust to a lower heat setting. (Stick with the stove if it doesn't.) If the Crème Anglaise starts to cook too quickly, simply lift the pot a few inches (about 7.5 cm) away from the heating element on the bottom of the pressure cooker housing.

COCONUT-PECAN FROSTING

A sweet buttery frosting loaded with coconut and pecans. A classic frosting for German chocolate cake.

2 tablespoons (28 g) unsalted butter

¼ cup (60 ml) evaporated milk

¼ cup (50 g) sugar

2 large egg yolks

½ cup (40 g) sweetened flaked coconut

⅓ cup (37 g) chopped pecans

¼ teaspoon vanilla extract

On the pressure cooking pot, select Sauté and add the butter to melt. Turn off the pressure cooker and whisk in the evaporated milk and sugar. Whisk in the egg yolks. Select Sauté and cook for about 2 minutes, whisking constantly, until the mixture comes to a boil and thickens. Using hot pads or silicone mitts, transfer the cooking pot from the pressure cooker housing to a heat-resistant surface. Stir in the coconut, pecans, and vanilla. Transfer to a storage container and cool to room temperature before using.

YIELD: 1 cup (about 280 g)

▶ **TIP:** For those of us who grew up on coconut-almond frosting, substitute ½ cup (46 g) sliced almonds for the chopped pecans.

CREAM CHEESE YOGURT FROSTING

This is an easy, perfectly sweet topping for anything from breakfast cake to cheesecake. Try it with the Carrot Cake Breakfast Cake (page 33) or the Sweet Peach Raspberry Swirl Breakfast Cake (page 37).

¼ cup (50 g) whipped cream cheese (see Tip)

¼ cup (60 g) plain Greek yogurt

1 to 2 tablespoons (15 to 28 ml) milk

3 tablespoons (24 g) powdered sugar

½ teaspoon vanilla extract

In a large bowl, combine the cream cheese, yogurt, milk, powdered sugar, and vanilla. Using a handheld electric mixer, mix the ingredients on medium speed until smooth. Refrigerate up to 1 week or until ready to use.

YIELD: ¾ cup (about 198 g)

> **TIP:** The whipped cream cheese is a little different than regular cream cheese. In a pinch, you can substitute regular cream cheese, but you may need to add a bit more milk to get the desired consistency. For a twist, make this frosting using one of the many fun flavors of whipped cream cheese available.

DULCE DE LECHE

Dulce de leche is similar to caramel. Making it in the pressure cooker is super easy—all you need is sweetened condensed milk! Drizzle it over your favorite dessert or just enjoy a spoonful to tame that sweet craving.

1 can (14 ounces, or 425 ml) sweetened condensed milk

8 to 10 cups (1.9 to 2.4 L) water

Equally divide the sweetened condensed milk between two half-pint (8 ounce, or 235 ml) canning jars. Place the lid on the jar and screw on the ring just until fingertip tight (when you start to feel resistance as you tighten).

Place a trivet in the bottom of the pressure cooking pot and place the filled jars on top. Add water to the cooking pot until it reaches halfway up the jars. Lock the lid in place and turn the pressure release valve to the Sealed position. Select High Pressure and 20 minutes cook time.

When the cook time ends, turn off the pressure cooker. Let the pressure release naturally for 15 minutes, and finish with a quick pressure release. When the valve drops, carefully remove the lid.

With canning jar lifter tongs, carefully remove the jars from the cooking pot. Let the jars cool for 10 minutes. Using hot pads or silicone mitts, open the lids. Whisk until smooth. Let cool.

Once cool, cover and refrigerate. Use within 1 week.

YIELD: 12 fluid ounces, about 1½ cups (355 ml)

> **TIP:** If you prefer, make this in a single 16-fluid ounce (475 ml) jar; it just takes longer to cook.

SALTED CHOCOLATE DULCE DE LECHE

A chocolatey twist on the ever-popular dulce de leche sauce. An extra pinch of salt makes the whole jar shine with sweet-and-salty flavors!

1 can (14 ounce, or 425 ml) sweetened condensed milk

1 ounce (28 g) high-quality semisweet or bittersweet chocolate, chopped

8 to 10 cups (1.9 to 2.4 L) water

½ teaspoon kosher salt

Pour the sweetened condensed milk into a pint-size (16 ounce, or 475 ml) canning jar. Place the chocolate on top and then place the lid on the jar, and screw on the ring just until fingertip tight (when you start to feel resistance).

Place a trivet in the bottom of the pressure cooking pot and place the filled jar on top. Add water to the cooking pot until it reaches halfway up the jar. Lock the lid in place and turn the pressure release valve to the Sealed position. Select High Pressure and 45 minutes cook time.

When the cook time ends, turn off the pressure cooker. Let the pressure release naturally for 15 minutes, and finish with a quick pressure release. When the valve drops, carefully remove the lid.

With hot pads or silicone mitts, carefully remove the jar from the cooking pot and cool for 10 minutes. Use the hot pads or silicone mitt to open the lids. Add the salt and whisk until smooth.

Once cool, cover and refrigerate. Use within 1 week.

YIELD: 12 ounces, about 1½ cups (355 ml)

> **TIP:** This recipe can be easily doubled or tripled for parties and gifts.

VANILLA WHIPPED CREAM

Whipped cream is one of the most versatile, well-known, and beloved dessert toppings! Although this recipe doesn't use the pressure cooker, because it is featured in so many of our recipes, we've included it here for easy access.

2 cups (475 ml) heavy cream

½ cup (60 g) powdered sugar

2 teaspoons vanilla extract

In a medium bowl, using a handheld electric mixer, beat the cream on medium-high speed until it starts to thicken. Add the powdered sugar and vanilla and continue to beat until stiff peaks form.

YIELD: 4 cups (240 g)

▶ **TIP:** If you need to make the whipped cream ahead of time, stabilize it! In a microwave-safe bowl, sprinkle 1 teaspoon unflavored gelatin over 1 tablespoon (15 ml) cold water. Let stand for 1 minute. Microwave at high power for 5 to 10 seconds until the mixture stars to foam and the gelatin dissolves. Let cool. Add the cooled gelatin to the whipped cream just before adding the vanilla and sugar.

TROPICAL SUGARED FRUIT

Simple ingredients turn into a sweet, syrupy topping. Try this fruit with the White Chocolate–Lime Rice Pudding (page 124) or on top of the Tropical Cheesecake (page 41).

½ cup (90 g) diced fresh mango

½ cup (85 g) diced fresh strawberries

½ cup (80 g) diced fresh pineapple

½ cup (90 g) diced fresh kiwi

Juice of ½ of a lime

2 tablespoons (26 g) sugar

In a small bowl, stir together the mango, strawberries, pineapple, kiwi, lime juice, and sugar. Let sit for at least 30 minutes before serving so the sugar has a chance to create a sweet fruit syrup. Stir the fruit and serve. Keep refrigerated for up to 1 day.

YIELD: 2 cups (370 g)

> **TIP:** Serve this with any brand of cinnamon sugar pita chips for an amazing appetizer.

CHERRY PIE FILLING

Kick your desserts up a notch by making your own pie filling. Frozen cherries are available year-round, so cherry desserts don't have to wait just for summer!

6 cups (840 g) frozen sweet cherries, divided

⅔ cup (134 g) sugar

2 tablespoons (28 ml) freshly squeezed lemon juice

¼ cup (32 g) cornstarch

¼ cup (60 ml) cold water

¼ teaspoon almond extract

In the pressure cooking pot, combine 4 cups (560 g) of the frozen cherries with the sugar and lemon juice. Stir to combine. Lock the lid in place and turn the pressure release valve to the Sealed position. Select High Pressure and 2 minutes cook time.

When the cook time ends, turn off the pressure cooker. Let the pressure release naturally for 15 minutes and finish with an intermittent pressure release, opening and closing the valve in regular intervals to reduce foaming or spitting. When the valve drops, carefully remove the lid.

In a small bowl, whisk the cornstarch and cold water. Add this slurry to the cherry mixture. Select Sauté. Bring the cherries to a boil, stirring constantly until the sauce thickens. Stir in the almond extract and remaining 2 cups (280 g) of frozen cherries. Pour the cherry filling into a storage container and cool to room temperature. Refrigerate until ready to use.

YIELD: 5 cups (700 g)

> **TIP:** This recipe makes enough pie filling for a 9-inch (23 cm) pie, the equivalent of two cans of pie filling. If you're making this as a topping for cheesecake or ice cream, divide the recipe in half.

NATURALLY SWEETENED CARAMEL APPLE PIE FILLING

This amazing pie filling comes together in minutes and uses only natural sweeteners!

4 pounds (1.8 kg) Honeycrisp apples

1½ cups (270 g) whole dates, pitted

1 teaspoon ground cinnamon

4 tablespoons (60 ml) apple juice, divided

1 tablespoon (8 g) cornstarch

Peel, core, and slice the apples about ¼ inch (6 mm) thick. Place the apples in a large bowl and set aside.

Use kitchen shears or sharp scissors to cut each date into six to eight pieces. Add the dates to the apples and sprinkle in the cinnamon. Toss to combine. Pour the apple mixture into the pressure cooking pot and add 2 tablespoons (28 ml) of apple juice. Lock the lid in place and turn the pressure release valve to the Sealed position. Select High Pressure and 2 minutes cook time.

When the cook time ends, turn off the pressure cooker. Use a quick pressure release.

In a small bowl, whisk the cornstarch with the remaining 2 tablespoons (28 ml) of apple juice. Select Sauté and bring the apples to a light simmer. Stir in the cornstarch slurry and cook, stirring, until the filling thickens.

Use hot in Caramel Apple Pie (page 95) or cover and refrigerate for up to 1 week.

YIELD: 8 cups (2 L)

> **TIP:** For this recipe, buy nine or ten large apples to ensure you have enough. Honeycrisp apples are the sweetest and retain their texture best when baked, but you could also use Pink Lady, Jonagold, Braeburn, or Granny Smith apples—or a mixture.

LEMON CURD

Lemon curd is sort of a soft, creamy, tart, buttery, sunny jam that packs a powerful pucker punch! Lemon lovers will want to put a little dollop on everything.

4 tablespoons (56 g) butter, at room temperature

⅔ cup (134 g) sugar

2 large eggs

½ cup (120 ml) freshly squeezed lemon juice

2 teaspoons grated lemon zest

In a large bowl, using a handheld electric mixer, mix the butter and sugar on medium-high speed until well blended. Add the eggs and beat for 1 minute. Add the lemon juice and mix until blended—the mixture will be lumpy. Transfer the butter mixture to the cooking pot. Select Sauté and cook for about 2 minutes, stirring constantly, until the mixture just comes to a boil.

Using hot pads or silicone mitts, remove the cooking pot and place it on a heat-resistant surface. Stir in the lemon zest. Transfer the curd to a glass container or bowl. Cover the top of the lemon curd with plastic wrap. Cool to room temperature. Refrigerate until ready to serve. The lemon curd will thicken as it cools.

YIELD: about 2 cups (448 g)

▶ **TIP:** Lemon curd lasts 1 to 2 weeks in the refrigerator and up to 2 months in the freezer.

STRAWBERRY PIE FILLING

This quick-and-easy strawberry pie filling uses both frozen and fresh strawberries. The frozen strawberries create the sweet filling that surrounds the fresh berries for double the strawberry flavor in every bite.

1½ cups (210 g) frozen sliced strawberries (see Tip)

½ cup (100 g) sugar

1 tablespoon (15 ml) freshly squeezed lemon juice

2 tablespoons (16 g) cornstarch

2 tablespoons (60 ml) cold water

1 tablespoon (14 g) unsalted butter

2 pints (580 g) fresh strawberries, sliced into large bite-size pieces

In the pressure cooking pot, combine the frozen strawberries, sugar, and lemon juice. Stir to combine. Lock the lid in place and turn the pressure release valve to the Sealed position. Select High Pressure and 2 minutes cook time.

When the cook time ends, turn off the pressure cooker. Let the pressure release naturally for 5 minutes, and finish with a quick pressure release. When the valve drops, carefully remove the lid.

In a small bowl, whisk the cornstarch and cold water. Add this slurry to the strawberry mixture. Select Sauté. Bring the strawberries to a boil, stirring constantly until the sauce thickens. Stir in the butter. Transfer the pie filling to a large bowl to cool.

Stir the fresh strawberries into the strawberry sauce. Refrigerate up to 1 week or until ready to serve.

YIELD: 4 cups (about 800 g)

► **TIP:** Frozen strawberries are generally frozen at their peak, so using frozen strawberries will result in a redder, more flavorful sauce. However, you can substitute fresh strawberries for the frozen if you prefer.

- ▶ PREP TIME: 2 minutes
- ▶ COOK TIME: 2 minutes
- ▶ TOTAL TIME: 20 minutes

TRIPLE BERRY PIE FILLING

This pie filling recipe uses a combination of fresh and frozen berries. Frozen berries are generally less expensive and break down more easily when cooked, while fresh berries have an irreplaceable taste and texture. Using a blend gives you the best of both worlds!

3 cups (420 g) frozen triple berry blend

½ cup (100 g) sugar

1 tablespoon (15 ml) freshly squeezed lemon juice

3 tablespoons (24 g) cornstarch

3 tablespoons (45 ml) cold water

1 cup (125 g) fresh raspberries

½ cup (73 g) fresh blueberries

In the pressure cooking pot, combine the frozen berries, sugar, and lemon juice. Stir to combine. Lock the lid in place and turn the pressure release valve to the Sealed position. Select High Pressure and 2 minutes cook time.

When the cook time ends, turn off the pressure cooker. Let the pressure release naturally for 10 minutes, and finish with a quick pressure release. Carefully remove the lid.

In a small bowl, whisk the cornstarch and cold water. Add this slurry to the cooked berry mixture. Select Sauté and bring the berries just to a boil, stirring constantly until the sauce thickens. Stir in the fresh raspberries and blueberries. Serve warm, or cool to room temperature and chill until up to 1 week or until ready to serve.

YIELD: 4 cups (620 g)

> **TIP:** The frozen berry blend we used includes blueberries, raspberries, and blackberries, but most berries will work in this recipe. Or, use one type of berry, such as blueberries, for a blueberry pie filling.

Acknowledgments

A huge thank you to Jennifer for her invaluable contribution to this cookbook.

A big thank you to my recipe testers Genene, Carol, Karen, and Jennifer. The recipes are better because of your insights.

To the members of the *Pressure Cooking Today* community, thank you for your support and advice and for joining me on this pressure cooking journey.

Finally, thank you to my husband, who helped me in the kitchen creating the recipes, and to my boys for being my taste testers.

—Barbara

Thank you to my husband and kids for so eagerly tasting all my creations and critiquing them so honestly.

Also, a big thanks to my mother and sisters, who never stop believing in me and encourage me to work hard.

Thank you to my wonderful friends and neighbors who helped me test recipes along the way. The quality of these recipes is greater because of all your love and support!

—Marci

About the Authors

Barbara Schieving lives in a suburb of Salt Lake City, Utah, with her husband of forty years, who is often in the kitchen with her. He likes to refer to himself as her "slicer and dicer." They have four grown children and two adorable grandsons. She is the creator of two popular recipe blogs: her pressure cooking site, www.PressureCookingToday.com, where she shares fabulous, family-friendly recipes for the electric pressure cooker/Instant Pot, and www.BarbaraBakes.com, where she shares her passion for baking. *Pressure Cooking Today* and *Barbara Bakes* receive more than 1.5 million page views each month. Over the past decade, her distinctive recipes and conversational style have earned her a dedicated readership across the globe. Barbara's popular cookbook, *The Electric Pressure Cooker Cookbook*, was released in November 2017.

Marci Buttars is the mother of one sweet little girl and two high-energy twin boys. She's married to her motorcycle dream man, and together they are raising their family in a small town in Utah. She earned a master's degree in nursing from Graceland University and currently works as a family nurse practitioner with an emphasis in pediatrics. She has a passion for health and wellness and enjoys teaching these skills to others. She also has a great excitement for cooking and enjoys experimenting with a variety of ingredients and ethnic foods. Marci shares her recipes on https://TIDBITS-Marci.com. She is also the author of a popular pressure cooker cookbook, *Master the Electric Pressure Cooker*, released in September 2017. Other hobbies include motorcycle adventures with her husband, running, arts and crafts with her children, and gardening.

Index

apple
  Caramel Apple Pie, 95
  Cranberry-Orange Poached Pears, 108
  Naturally Sweetened Caramel Apple Pie
    Filling, 151
  No-Sugar-Added Applesauce, 110

bananas
  Banana Boats, 111
  Banana Split Pie, 97
  Brown Sugar Banana Nut Bread, 28
  Chocolate Peanut Butter Lava Cakes with
    Brûléed Bananas, 60–61
blueberries
  Lemon Blueberry Bread Pudding, 119
  Triple Berry Pie Filling, 155
breads
  Brown Sugar Banana Nut Bread, 28
  Overnight Cinnamon-Pecan Monkey
    Bread, 36
  tips and tricks, 12
breakfast
  Brown Sugar Banana Nut Bread, 28
  Carrot Cake Breakfast Cake with Cream
    Cheese Yogurt Frosting, 31
  Cinnamon Roll Steel Cut Oats, 24
  Honey Orange Poppy Seed Breakfast
    Cake with Raspberry-Orange
    Sauce, 32
  Honey Vanilla Greek Yogurt, 26
  Orange-Cranberry Breakfast Risotto, 25
  Overnight Cinnamon-Pecan Monkey
    Bread, 36
  Pineapple Upside-Down Breakfast Cake,
    29
  Pumpkin-Chocolate Chip Breakfast
    Cake, 34
  Sweet Peach Raspberry Swirl Breakfast
    Cake, 35
  tips and tricks, 12
brownie mix, for Caramel Walnut Brownie
    Pudding Cake, 81

cake mix
  Chocolate Lover's Dream Cake, 82
  Chocolate-Raspberry Cake for Two, 80
  German Chocolate Cake, 86
  Lemon Poppy Seed Cake, 76
  Peach Cobbler, 113
  Raisin-Pecan Spice Cake with Dulce de
    Leche Drizzle, 79
  Vanilla Confetti Cheesecake, 44
cakes. See also lava cakes.
  Angel Food Cake, 77
  Berry Cherry Pudding Cake, 118

Caramel Walnut Brownie Pudding
    Cake, 81
Carrot Cake Breakfast Cake with Cream
    Cheese Yogurt Frosting, 31
Chocolate Lover's Dream Cake, 82
Chocolate-Raspberry Cake for Two, 80
Cinnamon Tres Leches Cake with
    Macerated Strawberries, 84–85
German Chocolate Cake, 86
Honey Orange Poppy Seed Breakfast
    Cake with Raspberry-Orange
    Sauce, 32
Lemon Poppy Seed Cake, 76
Pineapple Upside-Down Breakfast
    Cake, 29
Pumpkin-Chocolate Chip Breakfast
    Cake, 34
Raisin-Pecan Spice Cake with Dulce de
    Leche Drizzle, 79
Sweet Peach Raspberry Swirl Breakfast
    Cake, 35
tips and tricks, 14
caramel
  Banana Boats, 111
  Caramel Apple Pie, 95
  Caramel Pecan Cheesecake, 52
  Caramel Pots de Crème, 127
  Caramel Walnut Brownie Pudding
    Cake, 81
  Coconut Flan, 128
  Dark Chocolate Salted Caramel Lava
    Cakes, 62–63
carrots, for Carrot Cake Breakfast Cake
    with Cream Cheese Yogurt
    Frosting, 31
cheesecake
  Caramel Pecan Cheesecake, 52
  Classic Cherry Cheesecake, 40
  Japanese Cheesecake, 54
  Key Lime Cheesecake, 56
  Mini Lemon Cheesecakes in a Jar, 57
  Oreo-Chocolate Chip Mini
    Cheesecakes, 55
  Pumpkin Vanilla Layered Cheesecake
    with Maple Glaze, 46–47
  Red Velvet Cheesecake with Vanilla
    Yogurt Glaze, 48–49
  Strawberry Swirl Cheesecake with White
    Chocolate Ganache, 42–43
  tips and tricks, 12–13
  Triple Layer Chocolate Mint Cheesecake,
    50–51
  Tropical Cheesecake, 41
  Vanilla Confetti Cheesecake, 44–45

cherries
  Banana Split Pie, 97
  Berry Cherry Chia Compote, 132
  Berry Cherry Pudding Cake, 118
  Cherry Pie Filling, 150
  Classic Cherry Cheesecake, 40
  Double Crust Cherry Pie, 92
  Pineapple Upside-Down Breakfast
    Cake, 29
  Tropical Cheesecake, 41
chocolate
  Chocolate Ganache, 139
  Chocolate Peanut Butter Lava Cakes with
    Brûléed Bananas, 60–61
  Dark Chocolate Salted Caramel Lava
    Cakes, 62–63
  German Chocolate Lava Cakes, 66–67
  Pumpkin-Chocolate Chip Breakfast
    Cake, 34
  Salted Chocolate Dulce de Leche, 147
  S'more Lava Cakes, 68–69
  Triple Layer Chocolate Mint Cheesecake,
    50–51
chocolate chips
  Banana Boats, 111
  Chocolate Tapioca Pudding, 122
  Oreo-Chocolate Chip Mini Cheesecakes,
    55
  Pumpkin-Chocolate Chip Breakfast
    Cake, 34
  Red Velvet Cheesecake with Vanilla
    Yogurt Glaze, 48–49
  S'more Bread Pudding, 121
chocolate fudge topping, for Chocolate
    Lover's Dream Cake, 82
cobblers
  Peach Cobbler, 113
  tips and tricks, 17
cocoa powder
  Caramel Walnut Brownie Pudding
    Cake, 81
  Chocolate Lover's Dream Cake, 82
  Dark Chocolate Syrup, 136
coconut
  Coconut Custard Pie, 98
  Coconut Flan, 128
  Coconut-Pecan Frosting, 144
  German Chocolate Lava Cakes, 66–67
coconut, cream of, for Tropical
    Cheesecake, 41
coconut milk
  Cinnamon Vanilla Coconut Syrup, 135
  Coconut Flan, 128
  Dark Chocolate Syrup, 136

compote, as Berry Cherry Chia
    Compote, 132
condensed milk
    Coconut Flan, 128
    Cinnamon Tres Leches Cake with
        Macerated Strawberries, 84–85
    Dreamy Orange Pie, 102
    Dulce de Leche, 146
    evaporated milk compared to, 17
    Key Lime Cheesecake, 56
    Salted Chocolate Dulce de Leche, 147
cookies, Oreo (all flavor varieties)
    Mini Lemon Cheesecakes in a Jar, 57
    Vanilla Confetti Cheesecake, 44–45
    Oreo-Chocolate Chip Mini
        Cheesecakes, 55
    Red Velvet Cheesecake with Vanilla
        Yogurt Glaze, 48
    Strawberry Swirl Cheesecake with White
        Chocolate Ganache, 42
    Triple Layer Chocolate Mint Cheesecake,
        50–51
cookies, other
    Caramel Pecan Cheesecake, 52
    Pumpkin Vanilla Layered Cheesecake
        with Maple Glaze, 46–47
    Sweet Potato Pie, 99
    Tropical Cheesecake, 41
    Vanilla Almond Custard Pie with
        Macerated Raspberries, 104–105
cranberries
    Cranberry-Orange Poached Pears, 108
    Orange-Cranberry Breakfast Risotto, 25
cream cheese
    Caramel Pecan Cheesecake, 52
    Carrot Cake Breakfast Cake with Cream
        Cheese Yogurt Frosting, 31
    Cinnamon Roll Steel Cut Oats, 24
    Classic Cherry Cheesecake, 40
    Cream Cheese Yogurt Frosting, 145
    Japanese Cheesecake, 54
    Key Lime Cheesecake, 56
    Mini Lemon Cheesecakes in a Jar, 57
    Oreo-Chocolate Chip Mini
        Cheesecakes, 55
    Pumpkin Vanilla Layered Cheesecake
        with Maple Glaze, 46–47
    Red Velvet Cheesecake with Vanilla
        Yogurt Glaze, 48–49
    Strawberry Swirl Cheesecake with White
        Chocolate Ganache, 42–43
    tips and tricks, 12
    Triple Layer Chocolate Mint Cheesecake,
        50–51
    Tropical Cheesecake, 41
    Vanilla Confetti Cheesecake, 44–45
crème brûlée, as Vanilla Bean Crème
    Brûlée, 129
croissants, for Lemon Blueberry Bread
    Pudding, 119
custards
    Coconut Flan, 128
    Crème Anglaise, 143

tips and tricks, 17
Vanilla Bean Crème Brûlée, 129

evaporated milk
    Cinnamon Tres Leches Cake with
        Macerated Strawberries, 84–85
    Coconut-Pecan Frosting, 144
    condensed milk compared to, 17

frosting
    Chocolate Ganache, 139
    Coconut-Pecan Frosting, 144
    Cream Cheese Yogurt Frosting, 145
fruit desserts
    Banana Boats, 111
    Chocolate Ganache, 139
    Cranberry-Orange Poached Pears, 108
    No-Sugar-Added Applesauce, 110
    Strawberry Trifle, 112
    tips and tricks, 17
    Triple Berry Crisp, 115

graham cracker crumbs
    Banana Split Pie, 97
    Classic Cherry Cheesecake, 40
    Coconut Custard Pie, 98
    Dreamy Orange Pie, 102
    Key Lime Cheesecake, 56
    S'more Bread Pudding, 121
    S'more Lava Cakes, 68
    Strawberry Pie, 101

heavy cream
    Caramel Pecan Cheesecake, 52
    Caramel Pots de Crème, 127
    Chocolate Ganache, 139
    Chocolate Lover's Dream Cake, 82
    Coconut Custard Pie, 98
    Crème Anglaise, 143
    Lemon Blueberry Bread Pudding, 119
    S'more Bread Pudding, 121
    Strawberry Swirl Cheesecake with White
        Chocolate Ganache, 42–43
    Strawberry Trifle, 112
    Sweet Potato Pie, 99
    Vanilla Almond Custard Pie with
        Macerated Raspberries, 104
    Vanilla Bean Crème Brûlée, 129
    Vanilla Whipped Cream, 148
honey
    Banana Boats, 111
    Honey Orange Poppy Seed Breakfast
        Cake with Raspberry-Orange
        Sauce, 32
    Honey Vanilla Greek Yogurt, 26
    Strawberry Vanilla Honey Syrup, 138

kiwi, for Tropical Sugared Fruit, 149

lava cakes. See also cakes.
    Chocolate Peanut Butter Lava Cakes with
        Brûléed Bananas, 60–61

Dark Chocolate Salted Caramel Lava
    Cakes, 62–63
Dulce de Leche Lava Cakes, 65
German Chocolate Lava Cakes, 66–67
S'more Lava Cakes, 68–69
tips and tricks, 13–14
White Chocolate and Nutella Lava
    Cakes, 70
White Chocolate Macadamia Lava
    Cakes, 71
White Chocolate Peppermint Lava Cakes,
    72–73
lemon
    Berry Cherry Chia Compote, 132
    Cherry Pie Filling, 150
    Japanese Cheesecake, 54
    Lemon Blueberry Bread Pudding, 119
    Lemon Curd, 153
    Lemon Poppy Seed Cake, 76
    Mini Lemon Cheesecakes in a Jar, 57
    Strawberry Pie Filling, 154
    Triple Berry Pie Filling, 155
lime
    Key Lime Cheesecake, 56
    Tropical Sugared Fruit, 149
    White Chocolate-Lime Rice Pudding, 124

mangoes, for Tropical Sugared Fruit, 149
maple syrup
    Berry Cherry Chia Compote, 132
    Cinnamon Vanilla Coconut Syrup, 135
    Cranberry-Orange Poached Pears, 108
    Dark Chocolate Syrup, 136
    Pumpkin Vanilla Layered Cheesecake
        with Maple Glaze, 46–47
marshmallows
    S'more Bread Pudding, 121
    S'more Lava Cakes, 68–69
mixed berries
    Berry Cherry Chia Compote, 132
    Berry Cherry Pudding Cake, 118
    Japanese Cheesecake, 54
    Triple Berry Pie Filling, 155

Nuts
    Brown Sugar Banana Nut Bread, 28
    Caramel Pecan Cheesecake, 52
    Caramel Walnut Brownie Pudding
        Cake, 81
    Coconut-Pecan Frosting, 144
    German Chocolate Lava Cakes, 66–67
    Overnight Cinnamon-Pecan Monkey
        Bread, 36
    Raisin-Pecan Spice Cake with Dulce de
        Leche Drizzle, 79
    Triple Berry Crisp, 115
    White Chocolate and Nutella Lava Cakes,
        70
    White Chocolate Macadamia Lava
        Cakes, 71

oats
  Cinnamon Roll Steel Cut Oats, 24
  Triple Berry Crisp, 115
orange
  Cranberry-Orange Poached Pears, 108
  Dreamy Orange Pie, 102
  Honey Orange Poppy Seed Breakfast
    Cake with Raspberry-Orange
    Sauce, 32
  Orange-Cranberry Breakfast Risotto, 25
  Raspberry-Orange Yogurt Sauce, 142
  Strawberry Trifle, 112

peaches
  Peach Cobbler, 113
  Sweet Peach Raspberry Swirl Breakfast
    Cake, 35
peanut butter
  Banana Boats, 111
  Chocolate Peanut Butter Lava Cakes with
    Brûléed Bananas, 60–61
pears, for Cranberry-Orange Poached
    Pears, 108
peppermint candy, for White Chocolate
    Peppermint Lava Cakes, 72–73
pies
  Banana Split Pie, 97
  Caramel Apple Pie, 95
  Cherry Pie Filling, 150
  Coconut Custard Pie, 98
  Double Crust Cherry Pie, 92
  Double-Crust Piecrust, 91
  Dreamy Orange Pie, 102
  Naturally Sweetened Caramel Apple Pie
    Filling, 151
  Single-Crust Piecrust, 90
  Strawberry Pie, 101
  Strawberry Pie Filling, 154
  Sweet Potato Pie, 99
  tips and tricks, 14, 16
  Triple Berry Pie Filling, 155
  Vanilla Almond Custard Pie with
    Macerated Raspberries, 104–105
  Whole Wheat–Coconut Oil Single
    Piecrust, 94
pineapple
  Pineapple Sauce, 140
  Pineapple Upside-Down Breakfast
    Cake, 29
  Tropical Cheesecake, 41
  Tropical Sugared Fruit, 149
pressure cookers
  benefits of, 7
  buttons, 8–9
  cooking pot, 8
  float valve, 8
  housing, 8
  lid, 8
  natural pressure release, 10
  practice test, 10
  pressure release, 8
  quick pressure release, 10
  sealing ring, 8

specialty equipment, 18–19
terminology, 10
puddings
  Berry Cherry Pudding Cake, 118
  Caramel Pots de Crème, 127
  Caramel Walnut Brownie Pudding
    Cake, 81
  Chocolate Tapioca Pudding, 122
  Lemon Blueberry Bread Pudding, 119
  Fluffy Minute Tapioca Pudding, 123
  S'more Bread Pudding, 121
  tips and tricks, 17
  troubleshooting, 21
  Vanilla Bean Rice Pudding, 126
  White Chocolate–Lime Rice Pudding, 124
pumpkin purée
  Pumpkin-Chocolate Chip Breakfast
    Cake, 34
  Pumpkin Vanilla Layered Cheesecake
    with Maple Glaze, 46–47

raisins
  Carrot Cake Breakfast Cake with Cream
    Cheese Yogurt Frosting, 31
  Cinnamon Roll Steel Cut Oats, 24
  Raisin-Pecan Spice Cake with Dulce de
    Leche Drizzle, 79
raspberry
  Chocolate-Raspberry Cake for Two, 80
  Raspberry-Orange Yogurt Sauce, 142
  Sweet Peach Raspberry Swirl Breakfast
    Cake, 35
  Triple Berry Pie Filling, 155
  Vanilla Almond Custard Pie with
    Macerated Raspberries, 104–105
rice
  Orange-Cranberry Breakfast Risotto, 25
  Vanilla Bean Rice Pudding, 126
  White Chocolate–Lime Rice Pudding, 124

sauces
  Crème Anglaise, 143
  Dulce de Leche, 146
  Pineapple Sauce, 140
  Raspberry-Orange Yogurt Sauce, 142
  Salted Chocolate Dulce de Leche, 147
  tips and tricks, 17
  Tres Leches Sauce, 84–85
sour cream
  Chocolate-Raspberry Cake for Two, 80
  Classic Cherry Cheesecake, 40
  Coconut Custard Pie, 98
  German Chocolate Cake, 86
  Lemon Poppy Seed Cake, 76
  Mini Lemon Cheesecakes in a Jar, 57
  Oreo-Chocolate Chip Mini
    Cheesecakes, 55
  Raisin-Pecan Spice Cake with Dulce de
    Leche Drizzle, 79
strawberry
  Angel Food Cake, 77
  Cinnamon Tres Leches Cake with
    Macerated Strawberries, 84–85

Strawberry Pie Filling, 154
Strawberry Swirl Cheesecake with White
    Chocolate Ganache, 42–43
Strawberry Trifle, 112
Strawberry Vanilla Honey Syrup, 138
Tropical Sugared Fruit, 149
sweet potatoes, for Sweet Potato Pie, 99
syrups
  Cinnamon Vanilla Coconut Syrup, 135
  Dark Chocolate Syrup, 136
  Strawberry Vanilla Honey Syrup, 138
  Tropical Sugared Fruit, 149

tapioca
  Chocolate Tapioca Pudding, 122
  Fluffy Minute Tapioca Pudding, 123
tips and tricks, 11–13
troubleshooting, 20–21

white chocolate
  Strawberry Swirl Cheesecake with White
    Chocolate Ganache, 42–43
  Triple Layer Chocolate Mint Cheesecake,
    50–51
  White Chocolate and Nutella Lava
    Cakes, 70
  White Chocolate–Lime Rice Pudding, 124
  White Chocolate Macadamia Lava
    Cakes, 71
  White Chocolate Peppermint Lava
    Cakes, 72

yogurt
  Carrot Cake Breakfast Cake with Cream
    Cheese Yogurt Frosting, 31
  Cream Cheese Yogurt Frosting, 145
  Honey Orange Poppy Seed Breakfast
    Cake with Raspberry-Orange
    Sauce, 32
  Honey Vanilla Greek Yogurt, 26
  Pineapple Upside-Down Breakfast
    Cake, 29
  pressure cooker setting for, 9
  Pumpkin-Chocolate Chip Breakfast
    Cake, 34
  Pumpkin Vanilla Layered Cheesecake
    with Maple Glaze, 46–47
  Raspberry-Orange Yogurt Sauce, 142
  Red Velvet Cheesecake with Vanilla
    Yogurt Glaze, 48–49
  Strawberry Swirl Cheesecake with White
    Chocolate Ganache, 42–43
  Sweet Peach Raspberry Swirl Breakfast
    Cake, 35
  Triple Layer Chocolate Mint Cheesecake,
    50–51
  Vanilla Confetti Cheesecake, 44–45